DIPLOMA IN DIGITAL APPLICATIONS

D204: ICT in Enterprise

R.S.U. Heathcote

PAYNE-GALLWAY

www.payne-gallway.co.uk

Acknowledgements

Published by Payne-Gallway Publishers Limited
Payne-Gallway is an imprint of
Harcourt Education Ltd., Halley Court,
Jordan Hill, Oxford OX2 8EJ

Copyright© R.S.U. Heathcote 2006

First published 2006

10 09 08 07 06
10 9 8 7 6 5 4 3 2 1

British Library Cataloguing in Publication Data
is available from the British Library on request

ISBN 1 904467 68 7

ISBN 9 781904467 68 7

Copyright notice

Cover image© Richard Chasemore 2005

Design and Typesetting by Direction Marketing
and Communications Ltd

Printed by Printer Trento S.r.l

Ordering Information

You can order from:

Payne-Gallway,
FREEPOST (OF1771),
PO Box 381, Oxford OX2 8BR

Tel: 01865 888070
Fax: 01865 314029
E-mail: orders@payne-gallway.co.uk
Web: www.payne-gallway.co.uk

**We are grateful to the following
organisations for kind permission to use
copyright material:**

Technobile article by Jamil Shehadeh,
Copyright Guardian Newspapers Limited 2005.

The Helios logo is a registered trademark of
BP p.l.c, reproduced with permission.

Tower Bridge Exhibition advertisement,
reproduced with permission of the City of
London.

Visit London advertisement, reproduced with
permission of Visit London.

British Heart Foundation advertisement
'Reproduced courtesy of the British Heart
Foundation'.

Screenshot from http://www.pmcoffice.co.uk
by permission of A2B Office.

Microsoft, Excel, PowerPoint, Outlook, Word
and Windows are either registered trademarks
of Microsoft Corporation in the United States
and/or other countries.

Microsoft product screenshots reproduced
with permission from Microsoft Corporation,
p104-110.

Every effort has been made to contact
copyright owners of material published within
this book. We would be glad to hear from
unacknowledged sources at the earliest
opportunity.

Photo credits
p1 and p10   R.S.U. Heathcote

Contents

Introduction

About DiDA

DiDA (Diploma in Digital Applications) is a revolutionary series of qualifications launched by Edexcel in 2005, replacing GNVQ qualifications in ICT. As a suite of qualifications, it progresses from the:

- Award in Digital Applications (**AiDA**), consisting of module D201, to

- Certificate in Digital Applications (**CiDA**), consisting of module D201 plus one other module, to

- Diploma in Digital Applications (**DiDA**), consisting of modules D201 to D204.

Each module requires 90 guided learning hours.

The qualification places emphasis on real-life skills. All assessment is paperless: you will submit an electronic portfolio of work via Edexcel Online for on-screen moderation. A Summative Project Brief (SPB) is supplied each year by Edexcel via their website, which will guide you through a series of tasks to be performed.

About Module D204

This module is all about the use of ICT in the various stages of developing a brand new enterprise. You will learn how ICT can help you to formulate different ideas for a business, research possible customers and competitors, market your new business ideas and create budgets and cash flow forecasts. You will also learn how to give your business a corporate image which conveys the right message to the intended audience, how to communicate electronically with your stakeholders and create presentations which get across your message.

An important element of this course is teamwork. Most successful entrepreneurs work with a team, bouncing ideas off each other, reviewing each other's work and sharing the workload. This is emphasised throughout the book.

This is a practical book which, as well as giving tips on how to go about planning a successful enterprise, will give you the software skills that you need to present your ideas convincingly in an eportfolio. The sample eportfolio created to accompany this book can be downloaded from **www.payne-gallway.co.uk** by clicking on the relevant link in the DiDA section.

About this book

In this book you will learn exactly what is required to do well in the Edexcel SPB. Planning, research and documentation skills are all covered, and **Good Marks... Bad Marks...** sections at the end of specific chapters will help to ensure that you know what is required to achieve top marks.

Chapter 1 – Planning a project

The project

For this module you will be given a scenario by Edexcel. You will need to do some research on the topic set and then produce all of the plans, research and budgeting needed to start running a business. You will also need to decide upon a logo and create a corporate image for your company, which you will use on all company advertising, letterheads and the company website. All of these components will finally need to be presented in an eportfolio which will be assessed by the exam board. You will be expected to spend a minimum of 30 hours on the project.

In order to practise the skills required for the set project, you will work through a sample project of a similar nature in this book. You can view the sample SPB online at **www.payne-gallway.co.uk**; click on the relevant link in the DiDA section.

The finished eportfolio, similar to the one you will produce, is also online at **www.payne-gallway.co.uk**; click on the relevant link in the DiDA section.

The scenario

Imagine that you have had a great new business idea. Your idea is to provide a PC healthcheck service to the students, teachers and parents associated with your school or college. The service would involve going around to people's houses and performing tests on their computers with the aim of maximising their running speed, installing and running up-to-date virus checkers and removing spyware. You will also sell several smaller items related to your service such as screen wipes, mice and USB flash memory sticks as an additional revenue source. You can also install new hardware such as extra memory or a larger disk drive.

Much of the work on this project will be done within a team. Together you will need to agree on what must be done to investigate the viability of this idea.

> ## Note:
>
> When you submit your work in your eportfolio, your own individual contribution must be clearly identified and all judgements and conclusions reached must be your own.

You will need some funding to set up this project, so once you have finished your market research and developed a financial strategy using a spreadsheet, you will have to present your idea to a board of potential investors and persuade them to part with their cash!

Planning your project

For your course assessment, you will be showing the elements specified in the SPB in an eportfolio. You must also include some supporting evidence of work that you do on your own and as a team.

You must produce a detailed plan of how you will complete all the required tasks within the time allowed.

Before you start the plan:

- read through the project brief

- make a list of everything you have to do

- decide how long you think each element is going to take

- decide on the order in which the tasks need to be done

- decide at what points you need to get feedback and evaluate your work so far.

At regular intervals you must make sure that you are on schedule and if you are not, you must reschedule the remaining tasks into the time you have left to complete the project. **Keep a record of any changes made to your schedule.**

The project brief

The Edexcel SPB is specified on their website and is spread out over a number of pages. To find it go to **http://dida.edexcel.org.uk**. When the time comes for you to start the planning process, you will have to explore the website and make a list of what you need to do, similar to the list on page 3.

For this sample project the tasks are given and each one will be explained in more detail within later chapters in this book.

The following list shows the tasks that you must complete.

1. Produce a plan listing individual tasks and estimated completion dates.

2. Create an organised directory structure for your project files.

3. Produce a Mind Map of all your ideas to get a clear idea of what your business is going to do and what it is not.

4. Conduct some market research into the level of interest in your idea.

5. Construct a financial spreadsheet model of your projected revenues and expenses and calculate your predicted break-even point.

6. Present your proposals to the board of investors.

7. Develop a corporate identity and logo.

8. Produce your business documents.

9. Produce a website for your business.

10. Create the eportfolio.

11. Get feedback and evaluate the project.

Creating a project plan

Projects are unlikely to succeed unless they are properly planned. However, before you can start to plan, you have to be absolutely clear about the purpose of the project and what you are required to produce.

You should read the entire project brief first. There are a number of key questions you need to ask, including:

- What do I have to produce?
- What is it for?
- Who is the intended audience?
- When do I have to have finished it by?
- What resources can I use?
- How will the success of the project be judged?
- Who will review my work and when?

You could use Word or Excel to produce a plan. This is a skill you will have learnt in D201.

Tip:

It is vital for good marks that you create a plan and stick to it, updating it regularly after each task.

Task No.	Task	Subtask	Time allowed	Start Date	End Date	Class/ home	Group/Initials	Notes
1	Plan the project	Read the project brief				H	CB	
		Create an organised folder structure for the project files						
		Produce a plan listing individual tasks, subtasks, estimated completion dates, etc.						
	CHECKPOINT	***Check plan with teacher***						
2	Mind Mapping	Brainstorming session				C	GRP	
		Use software to create Mind Map				C	GRP	
3	Market Research	Design MR Questionnaire				C	GRP	
		Prooduce MR Questionnaire				H	RH	
		Get MR Questionnaire filled in				C/H	GRP	
	CHECKPOINT	***Check plan with teacher***						
4	Analysis	(fill in subtasks)						
5	Business Plan	(fill in subtasks)						

Figure 1.1: Project plan

Save the project plan. Each member of the group will need to make a second copy of their own, which they will annotate and amend as the plan changes throughout the project.

Keeping a diary

You should keep a project diary as a record of all that happens during your project. The diary should include comments on:

- changes you made to your plan
- your individual work and contribution to the team
- problems you have solved as a team or individually
- what needs to be done next.

You do not have to include this in the sample eportfolio but you may be asked to include a diary with the Edexcel eportfolio.

Software

We will be using the following software to accomplish this project.

Task	Software	Output
1	Word	Project plan
2	Windows Explorer	Directory structure
3	OpenMind	Mind Map
4	Word and Excel	Market research
5	Excel	Spreadsheet model
6	PowerPoint	Presentation of business proposal
7	Photoshop Elements	Design of logo
8	Word and Publisher	Business documents
9	Word	Marketing mailshot
10	Dreamweaver	Business website
11	Dreamweaver	eportfolio

Creating a directory structure

You will need to set up a folder structure to hold the various files that you will create.

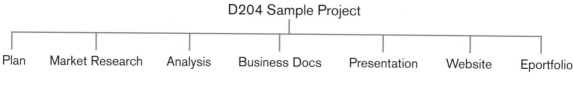

Figure 1.2: Folder structure

Use the folder structure above to create a directory structure in **Windows Explorer**. It should look like the one shown in Figure 1.3:

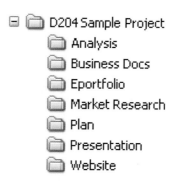

Figure 1.3: Folder structure

Good Marks... ✓

You will get good marks if you:

- read the SPB carefully and make a list of everything you need to do
- use a table, calendar or chart for your plan that includes:
  - task numbers
  - a description of each task
  - a description of each sub-task
  - time allowed for each task
  - the date you will start each task
  - the date you will finish each task
  - whether each task is done in class or at home
  - whether each task is done in a group or by a named individual
  - space for any notes relevant to each task
  - checkpoints, when you check your work with the teacher
  - extra time built in to your plan for emergencies or any problems
- agree your plan with your teacher
- keep a record of the changes you make to the plan
- monitor your progress and make sure you meet your deadlines
- keep a project diary of your day-to-day tasks.

Bad Marks... ✗

You will lose marks if you:

- set yourself an unrealistic timetable
- produce your plan but do not use it
- produce your plan *after* you have completed your project
- produce a plan that is the same as everyone else's.

Chapter 2 – Mind Mapping

The Mind Map concept

Mind Maps are the brainchild of Tony and Barry Buzan, and were introduced to the world in 1974. Written by them, *The Mind Map® Book* explains how to use this technique to assist with decision-making, organising your ideas, note-taking, creative thinking and brainstorming, and improving memory and imagination.

The Mind Map has five essential characteristics:

1. The subject of attention is crystallized in a central image.

2. The main themes of the subject radiate from the central image as branches.

3. Branches have a key image or key word printed on the associated line.

4. Topics of lesser importance are also represented as branches attached to higher level branches.

5. The branches form a connected nodal structure.

Using colour and pictures adds interest and turns the Mind Map into an individual work of art. Being creative with your Mind Map will help you to remember what it contains. For example, suppose you have to give a speech about your best friend (as, for example, the best man does at a wedding). You could use a Mind Map to help you come up with ideas.

 Get a blank piece of paper and a set of coloured felt pens. Put your friend's name in a coloured oval in the middle of the page, and then, using different colours, draw branches from the central 'node' and label them with possible topics that you could cover.

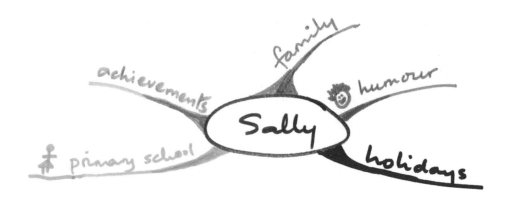

Figure 2.1: Example of a Mind Map

Extend the branches with more detailed ideas or reminders of anecdotes for each. For example, the Mind Map may continue something like this:

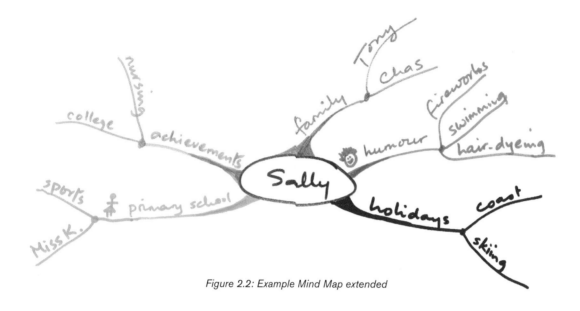

Figure 2.2: Example Mind Map extended

Exercise: Drawing a Mind Map

Try drawing your own Mind Map for one of the following topics:

- happiness
- what to do in the summer holidays
- your school/college
- your favourite school/college class
- your choice of career
- ideas for a business enterprise.

A big advantage of Mind Maps is that they allow you to put your ideas down within the order in which they occur to you, and by drawing a new branch in an appropriate place your ideas are automatically put into some kind of order.

Working in a group

In this module there is an emphasis on team working. You will work on your project in a group of three or four people, and hold regular meetings to plan each aspect of items that will go into the eportfolio. Some of the tasks will be carried out as a group, while others will be allocated to individuals within the group.

Most of the meetings will be held in class time. The following list contains some pointers for effective group working:

- **Appoint a group leader for each task**. This person should be responsible for thinking about the meeting beforehand, planning the agenda and leading the discussion.

- **Find out what each person in the group is good at and play to their strengths**. If one person is particularly good at graphics, perhaps he or she could be given the task of designing the logo.

- **Use the meetings to get feedback** from the rest of the group on your efforts so far. If someone has a good suggestion for improving the logo, for example, then it should be acted upon. Evidence of receiving and acting on feedback is required in the eportfolio.

- **Make notes on what was discussed** at each meeting and what tasks you have been allocated. These notes will form part of your project diary and will provide useful evidence for your eportfolio.

- **Use your plan** to make sure that you are on schedule. Stick to deadlines that you set at group meetings. If one person does not finish his or her allocated task it may put the whole group behind.

- **Make a note of your individual contribution** to each task. For example, you may have to include four templates in the eportfolio, only one of which you created yourself.

Exercise: Developing a business plan

Your group has decided that the business needs a front man to represent the company. This character could be either real or fictional. For the examples in this book, Colin Blake will front the company, which will be called **Colin's Computer Clinic**.

> ### Note:
>
> Whenever Colin is referred to in the rest of this book, the work can be divided up amongst the members of your group.

You are going to use Mind Mapping in order to come up with a business plan for **Colin's Computer Clinic**.

Write the title in the middle of the page. Then start letting questions and ideas form, writing them on branches of your Mind Map.

How will Colin market the company? How much money does he need to get started, and how much profit will he make?

You can use the following list to get you started. Some of the bullet points will be main branches and others will be sub-branches. Extend it as ideas come to you.

- What is the business all about?
- What goods or services will it provide?
- What is the demand for your product or service?
- Who are your likely customers?
- Where are they located?
- How much are they prepared to pay?
- What level of quality/service will they require?
- What is the competition for your product/service?
- How will you market your product or service?
- Are there changing trends and fashions that you should be aware of?
- What materials and supplies will you need, and where will you get them?

For top marks in one section of the D204 assessment, you have to use Mind Mapping software to generate and explore in depth three or more ideas for possible business opportunities.

In this chapter we will use **OpenMind** Mind Mapping software to create a Mind Map similar to the one below. Note that you can download a free trial version of this software from the **OpenMind** website at **www.matchware.net.**

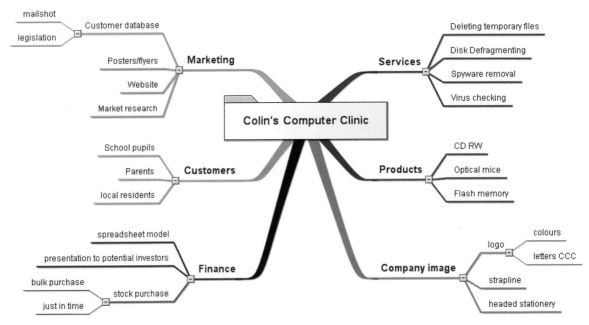

Figure 3.1: A Mind Map created in OpenMind

Starting OpenMind

⊙ Start **OpenMind** and in the dialogue box, select **New Document**.

⊙ With the **New Map** tab selected, select the **Mind Map** view (the default) and click **Open**.

A new map appears, with a root block ready for you to enter text.

Figure 3.2: Root block in OpenMind

▶ Type the text **Colin's Computer Clinic** and press **Enter**.

By default the Mind Map takes the name that you typed in the root, and you will see this name appear in the title bar at the top of the screen. The asterisk indicates that you have not yet saved it. Once you have saved and continued to work on the Mind Map, the asterisk will reappear to indicate that you have changed it since you last saved.

▶ Select **File**, **Save** or press the shortcut keys **Ctrl–S**. Save the file as **C3Mindmap** in the **Plan** folder that you should have already set up on page 6.

Inserting the main branches

Adding branches is very simple!

▶ Double-click on the root block.

A new branch appears with the word **idea** highlighted.

▶ Type the word **Services**.

▶ To add more branches press **Enter** again or, alternatively, double-click on the root. Enter branches for **Products**, **Customers** and **Marketing**.

Your Mind Map should look like Figure 3.3. If your branches appear in a different position it does not matter – you can edit it in a minute.

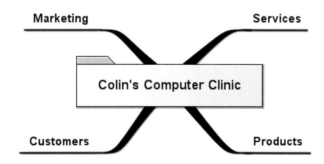

Figure 3.3: Starting to build the Mind Map

Editing and deleting branches

▶ To reposition a branch, drag its label to where you want the branch to appear.

▶ To delete a branch, click its label and press the **Delete** key.

▶ To edit a branch label, either double-click on it or click it once and press **F2**. Then you can edit the text.

Inserting sub-branches

The method for inserting sub-branches is almost exactly the same as the one that you used to insert main branches.

▶ Double-click the **Services** label and a new sub-branch appears. Type in **Deleting temporary files**.

▶ You can now add all the other branches and sub-branches, either by copying Figure 3.1 or using your own ideas.

Note that by clicking on the minus sign between a branch and sub-branch, you can collapse that branch. The figure below shows the Mind Map with two branches expanded and all the rest collapsed.

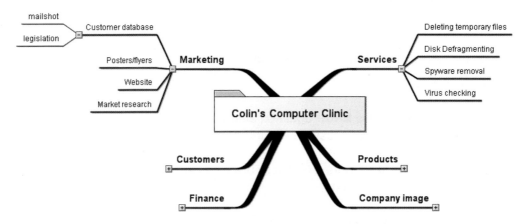

Figure 3.4: Expanded and collapsed branches

Adding colour

You can add lots of colour to your Mind Map. You can colour the branches, the text on separate branches, the background to text, and add coloured borders and backgrounds to a branch and all its sub-branches.

Colour is just one of the properties that you can set in the **Properties** panel, which is docked on the left of your screen.

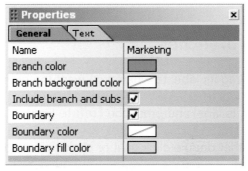

Figure 3.5: The Properties panel

You can set general properties and text properties for any branches selected.

- Select a single branch by clicking on its label. Select several branches and sub-branches by dragging a rectangle around or through the branches that you want to select.

- Restore all the sub-branches so that everything is visible. Try selecting the **Marketing** branch and all of its sub-branches by using the mouse pointer to drag out a rectangle.

- Click the **Branch color** property. A **Color** dialogue box appears.

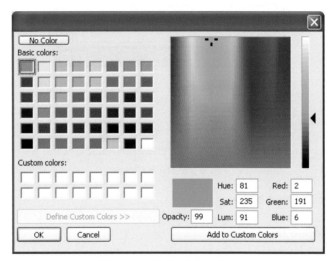

Figure 3.6: Color dialogue box

- Select a green colour. You can vary the shade using the slider on the right of the panel. When you are happy with the colour, click **OK**.

- Experiment with the options in the **Properties** panel to change text and branch colours. You can set a boundary fill colour like the one shown in Figure 3.7 by selecting the **Marketing** branch label and filling in the options as in Figure 3.5.

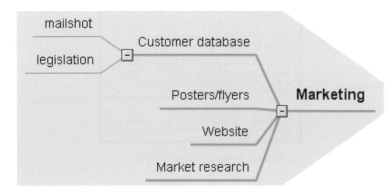

Figure 3.7: Setting a boundary fill colour

Inserting pictures

Pictures add interest and help you to remember your ideas when you don't have the Mind Map in front of you. We will insert a picture in the root block.

 Click in the **Search catalog** field of the **Media Catalog** (above the **Properties** panel) and type **computer**.

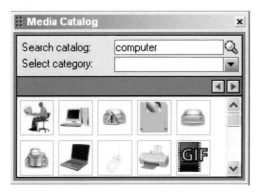

Figure 3.8: Media Catalog

 Drag a picture onto the root block.

The **Insert Picture** dialogue box appears.

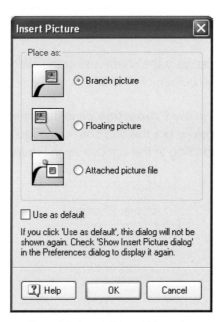

Figure 3.9: Insert Picture dialogue box

 Leave **Branch picture** selected and click **OK**.

The picture will be inserted and you can adjust its size if you wish.

Try inserting a suitable picture on one of the other branches. If you make the picture a **Floating picture**, you can move it around. Experiment with different options. You will see that if you specify **Attached picture file**, a green dot will appear to show that something is attached to the box. Clicking on the green dot opens the object in a **Picture Viewer**.

Inserting a text note

You can attach a text note to any branch or sub-branch.

⊚ Select the **just in time** branch at the bottom left of the Mind Map.

⊚ In the **Text note editor**, type in the text shown within Figure 3.10 below.

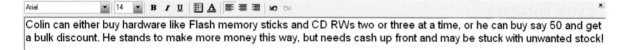

Figure 3.10: Text note editor

You can format the text using the toolbar above the **Text note editor** (shown in Figure 3.10) if you wish.

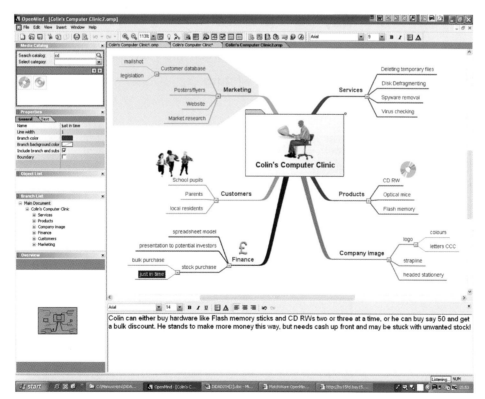

Figure 3.11: Formatting text

When you press **Enter**, you will see that a green dot appears beside the branch label to show that the branch has an attached object. If you hover the mouse over the green dot, a text note icon appears and you can click on this to see the text.

Inserting a comment

We will insert a comment, rather than a text note, on the **bulk purchase** branch.

Right-click the **bulk purchase** label and select **Insert** from the pop-up menu. Next, select **Comment**. Type a suitable comment and then click away from the box.

An unfilled circle appears, and when you hover the mouse over it, the comment pops up.

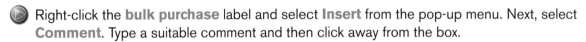
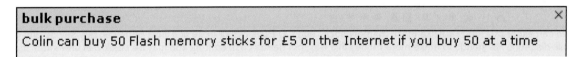

Figure 3.12: A comment box

Save your Mind Map again, this time with a different version number (e.g. **C3Mindmap2**) so that you will be able to show how you developed it.

Exporting your Mind Map as a picture

You can export your Mind Map as a **JPEG** file for insertion into your eportfolio.

From the menu bar select **File**, **Export to**, **Picture**.

The Picture Export dialogue box will appear.

Figure 3.13: Exporting to a picture file

● Navigate to the folder where you want to save the file. A **JPEG quality** of **60%** is probably good enough – you can preview it by pressing the **Preview** button. A higher percentage makes the file quality better but the file size larger.

● Click **Export**.

The Branch List

The **Branch List** shows a list of all the branches and sub-branches within the same format as Windows Explorer, and branches can be both expanded or collapsed in this window. The branches are shown in the order they appear in the Mind Map, starting at 'one o'clock' and working clockwise around the map.

Figure 3.14: The Branch List

You can change the order of the branches by dragging a branch in this list to a new position.

● Try dragging **Products** above **Services**.

You can manually adjust the layout by first turning off **Auto-layout**.

● Select **View** from the menu bar and deselect **Auto-layout**.

Note that if you re-enable **Auto-layout** again whilst working on your map, the main branches will be repositioned back in their default position. (You can then use **Undo** to cancel the re-enabling and revert to your custom layout.)

● To view a single branch of your Mind Map, click the branch name in the **Branch List**. This enables you to concentrate on just one aspect of the map.

● To re-display the whole map, right-click in the workspace and select **Show Complete Map**. Alternatively, click the name of the root in the **Branch List**.

The Overview panel

Dragging the grey box in this panel moves the Mind Map in the main window. This is a useful way of navigating around a very large Mind Map.

Exporting to PowerPoint

You can export your Mind Map into **PowerPoint**, where it can be fine-tuned. Before exporting you may wish to exclude certain branches from the export and can do this by disabling the **Include branches and subs in export** in the **Properties** panel.

For example, suppose we decide to exclude from the export the **Company image** branch and the sub-branches of **Marketing**.

The slides will appear in the order shown in the **Branch List**.

 Select the **Company image** branch.

 Click the **Include branch and subs in export** in the **Properties** panel to deselect it.

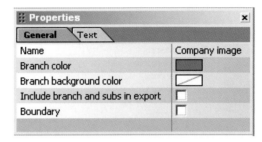

Figure 3.15: Include branch and subs in export

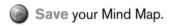 Similarly, select in turn each of the sub-branches of **Marketing** (starting with the **Customer database** branch) and deselect the **Include branches and subs in export** in the **Properties** panel for each one.

 Save your Mind Map.

There are two exporting methods available – **Quick Export** mode and **Advanced Export** mode. These allow you to choose a **PowerPoint** template for your presentation and to specify how the elements of your map should be treated.

We will just do a **Quick Export** here but you can experiment with the **Advanced Export** if you wish.

 From the menu bar select **File**, **Export to**, **Microsoft PowerPoint**, **Quick Export**.

Your presentation will appear within **PowerPoint** as in Figure 3.16. You will see that a slide is created for every branch and sub-branch (except those you specified that were not to be exported).

You will also note that, although no slide is created for **Company image**, the branch name appears on the first slide. You would need to delete this in **PowerPoint**.

Graphics and text need to be repositioned. Comments attached to a branch appear as **Speaker Notes** in the presentation.

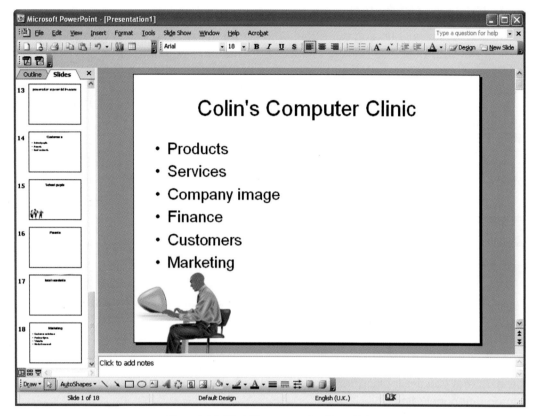

Figure 3.16: Mind Map exported to PowerPoint

Using Mind Maps as a planning tool

You may find that Mind Maps are a useful planning tool for many aspects of this course. When exploring different business opportunities, you will probably find it best to draw a separate Mind Map for each of your ideas.

Pack and Go

This is a useful feature that enables you to consolidate all of the external files referenced by attached objects in one folder, and optionally, compress it to a zipped folder. You could then, for example, e-mail the zipped folder to yourself, if you wish to continue working on the Mind Map at home.

 Make sure your Mind Map is saved.

 From the menu bar select **File**, **Pack and Go**. Then select one of the options. The third option creates a new Mind Map option, integrating all of the external files referenced in the original Mind Map within the **.omp** file, placing it in the output folder specified.

Types of market research

Market research is aimed at finding out about your target market in order to give you some idea of whether or not your business is likely to succeed. There are two different types of research: primary and secondary. Companies usually carry out secondary research first, which involves making use of data that has already been collected by other organisations.

Primary research

Primary research is the act of collecting data that is tailored to answering the questions that you have set about your company. For example, this may be in the form of a questionnaire.

Tip:

For top marks in this section you need to use at least three different sources of research including both secondary and primary data.

Secondary research

Secondary research is usually the easiest and least time-consuming of the two research types since the data that you are looking for already exists. There are various places where you can access information including:

- libraries – look for reference books containing statistical data
- magazines – often contain results of surveys they have collated
- wholesalers – find out the potential costs of your stock
- competitors – look at what they are doing and at what price
- government departments – find out about local demographics
- Internet – many of these useful sources will also be available online.

You will have to select the most appropriate secondary sources by asking questions such as:

- Is it biased?
- Is the information reliable and up-to-date?
- Can it be trusted?

Tip:

Your secondary data is often someone else's primary data! They may have collected it for their own research purposes.

Research topics

Size of the market

First of all you need to find out how big your potential market is – how many people might use your service or buy your products?

Your group is aiming to provide a computer health check service for pupils and parents associated with your school. It would be a good idea to find out how many pupils there are at the school and the number of pupil families that live within the school's local catchment area, where it is easy for Colin to get to them. The school's admissions secretary would probably be willing to provide this information.

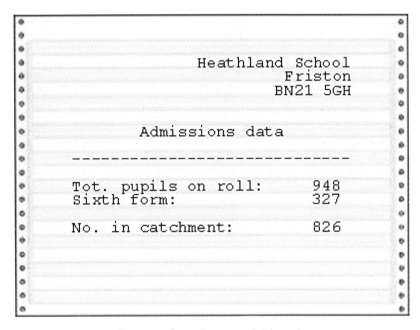

```
                    Heathland School
                           Friston
                        BN21 5GH


                 Admissions data

         ------------------------------------

      Tot. pupils on roll:        948
      Sixth form:                 327

      No. in catchment:           826
```

Figure 4.1: Secondary research information

The potential need

You must find out if there is a need for your products or services, or if you can create a need through advertising and marketing. People often don't realise that they need something until it is invented, for example, nobody needed a mobile phone until they came along. People may not know that they need a flash memory stick until you persuade them of the benefits.

You may be able to find articles in magazines or newspapers that indicate there is a potential need for the type of service that you intend to provide.

On the next two pages there are two articles, one from *The Guardian* and the other from PC World's free magazine.

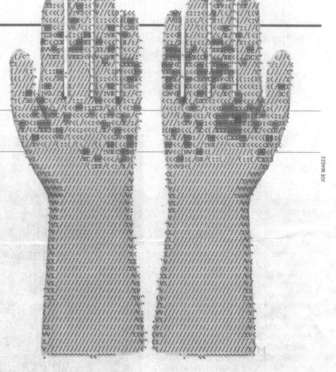

The Guardian | Thursday November 3 2005

Technobile

Don't curse your computer for crashing – curse yourself for bad housekeeping

No matter what the marketing men tell us, computers are complex and fragile. They can't really look after themselves.

"I know what the problem was now: viruses."

"How many viruses do you have?"

"Seventeen."

"How did you manage that?"

"The bloody thing wasn't updating."

A familiar tale. My friend's antivirus program had indeed stopped updating its database of known threats, but he was unaware. As a consequence, the operation of his PC had slowed to a crawl, then a halt.

A cursory glance every week or so at the status of his antivirus program would have saved him, and me, many hours of frustration. A friend in need... he'll certainly be busy when he eventually gets up and running again.

It's important to realise that like a car, your computer needs regular servicing if you want it to stay in tip-top condition. Without regular checks, it will eventually break down, sometimes taking all your important data with it. More often than not, your computer has stopped working because you didn't look after it. You just wanted it to work.

Maybe you are quite diligent with regard to your computer housekeeping, but then through no fault of your own you fell foul of a hard disk failure. But

it's OK, because you'll just refer to your backup, right?

"I lost all my MP3s last week when my drive failed," grinned another friend a month ago. He smirked because he knew that the loss of his files would annoy me more than it did him. If he wasn't bothered, I shouldn't have been. But I was.

It's all so silly: trouble-free computing is simple. Enable your automatic update program, get a free software firewall and some antivirus software. Then download a program to deal with adware and spyware. All that is required is 10 minutes each week to check they're up to date and doing their bit.

Finally, regular backups. Most new computers have built-in DVD writers, but even external ones come in at under £40,

or you could even use a USB flash drive.

So, no excuses then. If you don't treat backing-up as a priority and you find that your "stupid" computer keeps dying, along with all your files, just ask yourself one question. Could I have avoided those hours of cursing and crawling around under my desk?

If you still can't be bothered, close down all your programs, turn off the computer and put it back in its box. Then go out and buy yourself a leather-bound ledger for your accounts. Ledgers are great because they don't need to be serviced and they definitely don't get viruses. Better still, get an abacus.

Then you can work out how much time your "stupid" computer was saving you. **Jamil Shehadeh**

Figure 4.2: Secondary research on the need for your services (copyright Guardian Newspapers Limited 2005)

PC World has a wealth of information on their 'healthcheck' service, available in their stores and online. It is also worth visiting other websites that review services such as these to get an idea of their opinion, especially if they are comparing such services with others they have looked at.

You can also find useful reviews of this service online to see how previous customers found it. Print out any useful information you find for easy reference later on. The printout will include the source and date on it as well, to help you with your acknowledgements.

Know How

The importance of
Keeping your PC clean

MAKE SURE YOU OPTIMISE YOUR PC'S PERFORMANCE WITH THIS ESSENTIAL GUIDE TO CARE AND CLEANING

Ensuring your PC is clean and tidy isn't just about keeping up appearances. Care and attention could extend your computer's lifespan, improve performance and even make for a healthier home environment in your home or office.

The inevitable truth is PCs attract dirt, especially when they are placed on the floor or if you have pets. Dust, hair and even living bugs can get into your PC and lodge on your accessories – ignore them, and they might just cause you a serious problem.

You should begin by keeping an eye on your PC itself – the fan at the rear can become clogged with dirt and dust, which can cause your machine to overheat if left unchecked. It pays to periodically dust off your base unit or to mop it with an alcohol-free wipe to reduce clogging (remember to turn off all power to your PC first, of course).

Prevention

It's not just your base unit that needs a little TLC, however: your keyboard, monitor, mouse and other accessories should also be kept in tip-top condition.

These days you can invest in an optical mouse – which has no working parts – to keep your mouse pointer running smoothly. If you do have a rollerball mouse, periodically removing the ball and wiping it with a damp cloth, or better still an alcohol-free wipe, should prevent performance problems.

Keyboards too, can become sticky and even stop functioning if neglected but luckily there are plenty of products on the market to ensure you don't face the cost of replacing your kit after an unfortunate spillage or an excessive build up of dust.

Of course, prevention is often better than cure, and the products listed here will definitely help. ◘

Figure 4.3: An article from PC World magazine

Competition and similar companies

You should perform some research into other companies that offer similar or complimentary products and services. These might be in direct competition with your idea or in an entirely different area. Their product may even help you to reach your own market, for example, a seed company might advertise in a garden furniture catalogue.

Here is part of a flyer advertising related services.

Cosí Media
Communicate With Technology

Cosí Media recognise that attending computer courses can be time consuming, expensive and unnecessary; especially when all you need is someone to sit with you and guide you in a clear and uncomplicated way. Using technology can be both frustrating and confusing, but what Cosí Media do differently is to walk you through it step-by-step at a pace that suits you.

Cosí Media specialise in two main areas:

One-to-one help with 'simple' technology use in your own home:

PC installation, advice on new equipment, word processing, e-mails, internet, anti-virus (PC clean-up), digital photos, image manipulation, online music and much, much more...!

Figure 4.4: A flyer from a similar company

Costs

Colin will also need to know how much he will have to pay for his stock in order to calculate whether he can make a realistic profit from it. This information can be found on the Internet from PC equipment wholesalers. Using the Internet he will be able to look up wholesale and individual item costs from many wholesalers and retailers around the country.

Colin is thinking of selling flash memory sticks, screen wipes and optical mice as well as offering the healthcheck service. Through various searches using www.google.com, several good prices were found for all products:

USB drives	*128Mb £9.99*
	256Mb £12.99
Screen wipes	*£2.13 for 20 or*
	£5.82 for 100
Optical mice	*£16.99*

Figure 4.5: Product costs found on the Internet

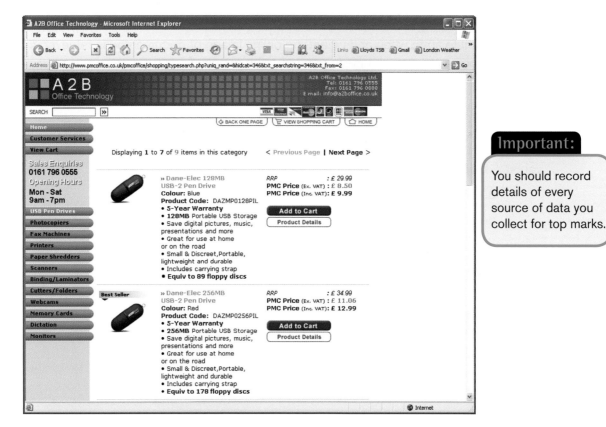

Figure 4.6: Internet research

Important:

You should record details of every source of data you collect for top marks.

It would also be useful to find out how much other companies are charging for these items and what sort of services Colin's competitors offer. Local computer stores will sell all these products and may also offer a PC healthcheck service. A member of your group could go along posing as a potential customer and collect some information or leaflets from them.

Acknowledging your sources

It is essential to record the sources of your information, both primary and secondary.
All references need to be written in a particular way. It is recommended that you keep a list of references throughout the project so that you can list them all in your eportfolio at the end. This will help you to get top marks.

Books should be referred to like this:

* Heathcote, R. (2005) *DiDA D201 Using ICT*, Payne-Gallway Publishers, pp. 194–195.

Documents retrieved from websites should be referred to like this:

* WWF *Living Planet Report 2004,* retrieved January 18, 2005, from
  http://www.wwf.org.uk/filelibrary/pdf/lpr2004.pdf

Or if you have used an online image:

* Description of title or image. (online image) Available http://address/filename.extension, date of document or, if not available, date of download.

It is important to state when and where the online image or document was retrieved from because web pages may change in content or be removed.

Collecting primary data

Primary data is collected by you and is more specific to your business than secondary research. This type of data may not have been collected before so you will have to go out and collect it yourself. Methods of collecting primary data are:

* questionnaires – by post, in the street or by phone
* personal interviews
* focus groups
* observation.

 **Question:**

What are the advantages and disadvantages of each of these methods of primary data collection?

In Chapter 5 we will plan and design a questionnaire which will be given out or sent to your potential customers.

Good Marks... ✓

You will get good marks if you:

- use Mind Mapping software to organise your ideas for the proposed business

- do some thorough research on the viability of your business idea, using several different secondary sources

- do some primary research to find out what other people, including potential customers, think of your idea.

Bad Marks... ✗

You will lose marks if you:

- make up your research data

- continue developing the business even when your research shows it is unlikely to be successful.

Chapter 5 – Designing a questionnaire

Planning a questionnaire

For **Colin's Computer Clinic**, a questionnaire will be handed out to pupils at the school for them to fill out at home and bring back a few days later.

The important thing to remember when designing your questionnaire is to have a clear idea of what information you want to find out, so that you can construct your questions effectively. You want to make sure that you have included everything you will need without going overboard. You don't want to hand out the questionnaire and later find that you forgot something. On the other hand, you don't want to be swamped with too much data to analyse.

You must devise a set of unambiguous questions to ask people, and decide which people to ask and how.

If you are planning to do a survey, you must design a questionnaire that:

- collects all the data you need
- does not influence the responses people give
- records the data in a format that is easy to analyse
- is easy to complete.

For this project you could decide to collect the following data:

- names, addresses and e-mail addresses to put in a customer database – this will be useful in order to contact your customers and to send out marketing mailshots (it might also be useful to collect their telephone numbers!)
- number of PCs that the average customer owns
- how old their computers are
- whether or not they already have a flash memory stick
- whether or not they see a need to speed up their computers
- whether or not they would be interested in a low-cost healthcheck service.

You might want to ask other questions to find out more about peoples' ages, gender, etc. However, in this example, this is not so important.

Asking the right people

Imagine that you wanted to find out how many people in the UK felt that there was too much football shown on TV. You would get two very different responses if you handed out the questionnaires at a football match and in an old people's home.

It is important to select your group of respondents carefully in order to ensure that the answers accurately reflect the views of your target population.

Creating the survey

You are going to use **Microsoft Word** to create the questionnaire shown in Figure 5.1.

Market Research Survey

I am setting up a computer health check service to keep your PC running smoothly. This service will include virus checking and removal, blocking pop-up advertisements whilst on the Internet and removing unwanted spyware. I will also help speed up your PC by removing old and temporary files that accumulate quickly, and by rearranging the way your files are stored on your hard disk. All this will be done in a quick home visit by prior arrangement.

Please will you take a minute to fill in and return this short questionnaire.

Title (Mr, Mrs, Ms): _____   First name: _____

Surname: _____

Address: _____

Postcode: _____   EMail: _____

Q1:   How many PCs do you have at home? ____

Q2:   For each of these PCs please state their age in years: PC1? ____

PC2? ____

PC3? ____

Q3:   Do you currently own a USB Flash Memory Stick?   Yes ☐   No ☐

Q4:   Do you feel that your computer has become slower since you bought it?

Yes ☐   No ☐

Q5:   Would you be interested in this kind of service for only £10 per PC?

Yes ☐   No ☐

Thank you for filling in this questionnaire, which will earn you a 10% discount on your first service booked before February 28th. Please return it to 21 Bishop Road, Friston BN21 3TU.

C Blake

Colin Blake, Managing Director

Your details will be stored on a computer to help with the smooth running of the business. They will not be passed to anyone else for any purpose whatsoever. Please tick here if you do not want your details held. ☐

Figure 5.1: An example market research questionnaire

Setting the margins in a new document

🔘 Open a new document in **Word**.

🔘 From the menu, select **File**, **Page Setup**. You will see the following screen.

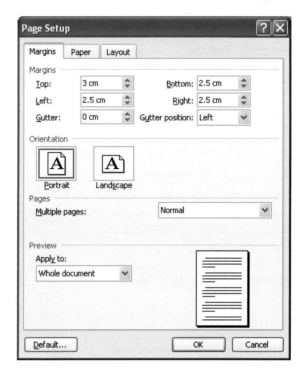

Figure 5.2: Setting margins in a Word document

🔘 Set the **Top** margin to **4 cm** and all the other margins to **3 cm**. Then click **OK**.

Using existing styles

For the heading you can use one of **Word**'s built-in styles called **Heading 1**.

🔘 On the **Formatting** toolbar, click on the drop-down arrow in the **Style** box.

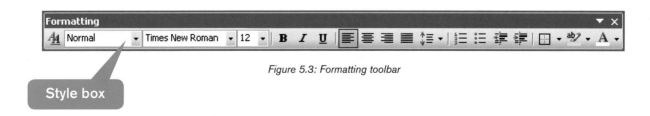

Figure 5.3: Formatting toolbar

Style box

Select the style **Heading 1** from the drop-down list of styles.

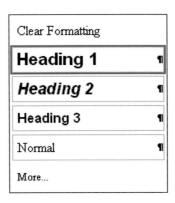

Figure 5.4: Drop-down list of styles

Enter the text **Market Research Survey** and press **Enter** twice. Notice that the style box now says **Normal**, because that is the style that will follow **Heading 1** by default.

Enter the first 10 lines of text as shown in Figure 5.1, until you get to the start of the first question. Use the **Underscore** key (next to the **zero**; hold down **Shift** while pressing it) to create the lines.

Format the text as **Arial**, size **11**.

Creating a new style

We will create a new style for the questions. The font for the new style will be **Arial**, size **11** and will have a 'hanging indent' so that text lines up neatly, as in Q3 of the survey.

On a new line, type the following text (press the **Tab** key after **Q1:**).

Q1: How many PCs do you have at home?

From the **Format** menu select **Styles and Formatting**. You will see a **Styles and Formatting** pane appear on the right of the screen.

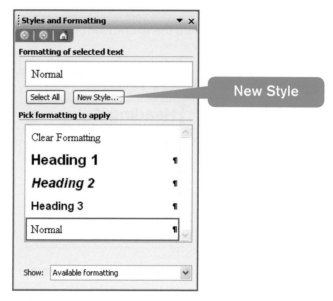

Figure 5.5: Styles and Formatting pane

⊚ Click the **New Style** button.

⊚ In the **New Style** window, give the style the name **Question** and specify that as the style for the following paragraph. Do not select **OK** yet.

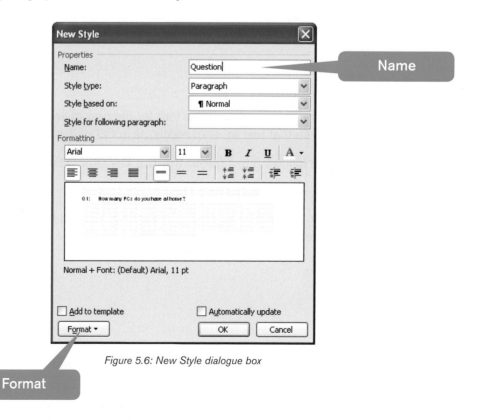

Figure 5.6: New Style dialogue box

- Click the **Format** button and select **Paragraph**; this brings up the **Paragraph** dialogue box. Create a hanging indent at **1 cm** as in Figure 5.7.

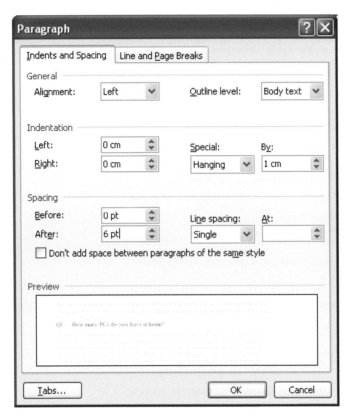

Figure 5.7: Paragraph dialogue box

- Increase the **Spacing After** to **6** points.

- Click **OK**, and **OK** in the next window.

- Click in the left margin next to the question to select the text, then click in the **Style** box to select your new **Question** style.

- Enter the next two questions as shown in Figure 5.8.

- At the end of question 3 press the **Tab** key and type **Yes**.

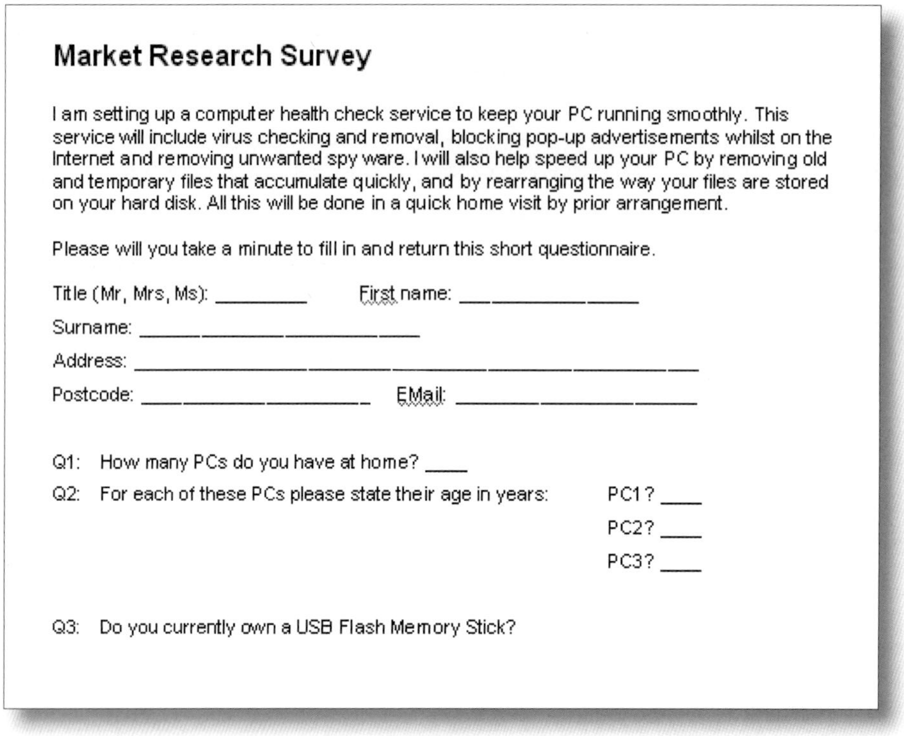

Market Research Survey

I am setting up a computer health check service to keep your PC running smoothly. This service will include virus checking and removal, blocking pop-up advertisements whilst on the Internet and removing unwanted spy ware. I will also help speed up your PC by removing old and temporary files that accumulate quickly, and by rearranging the way your files are stored on your hard disk. All this will be done in a quick home visit by prior arrangement.

Please will you take a minute to fill in and return this short questionnaire.

Title (Mr, Mrs, Ms): _____   First name: _____

Surname: _____

Address: _____

Postcode: _____   EMail: _____

Q1:   How many PCs do you have at home? ____

Q2:   For each of these PCs please state their age in years: PC1? ____

                                                                                                       PC2? ____

                                                                                                       PC3? ____

Q3:   Do you currently own a USB Flash Memory Stick?

Figure 5.8: Questions 2 and 3

Inserting a special symbol

Next you need to insert the little square for people to tick.

From the **Insert** menu select **Symbol**; the **Symbol** dialogue box appears.

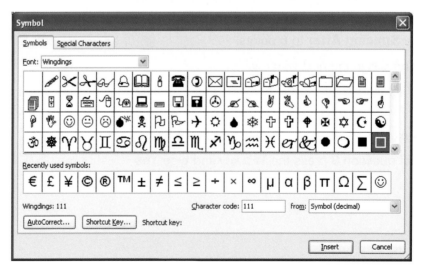

Figure 5.9: Symbol dialogue box

Find the little square (see Figure 5.9) and click **Insert**. You may need to select **Wingdings** from the **Font** drop-down menu if it has not appeared automatically.

 Press the **Tab** key to tab across and type **No**. Add another tick box. Note that you should always use tabs rather than spaces to ensure that text lines up properly.

Now complete the rest of the questionnaire so that it looks like the one in Figure 5.1.

Analysing the results of the survey

Once you have handed out questionnaires and collected in those that have been completed, you must save the results of the survey in a spreadsheet. In D201 you learnt how to analyse the results of a similar questionnaire. This type of analysis will not form part of this sample project. You may be asked to include the results of your research in the Edexcel SPB.

Exercise 1: Designing a spreadsheet

Design a spreadsheet to hold all the data from the completed questionnaires. The data that you collect should include the name and address details of all the people who completed the questionnaire, as well as their answers to the questions.

Gather some data from classmates and put the data in your spreadsheet. Your spreadsheet will look something like the one in Figure 5.10.

	A	B	C	D	E	F	G	H	I	J	K	L
1	Title	FirstName	Surname	Address1	Address2	Town	Postcode	email	PCs	FlashDrive	Slower	Service
2	Mrs	Constance	Corbett	17 Long Street		London	SW4 7RF	c.corbett@talk21.com	1	Yes	Yes	Yes
3	Mrs	William	Melsa	27 Pearcroft Drive		London	SW4 2TH	willmelsa@ntlworld.com	2	No	Yes	Yes
4	Mrs	Sharon	Maxfield	145 Helsden Rd		London	SW3 7YP	bigsharon@yahoo.co.uk	1	No	No	No
5	Mrs	Deidre	Griffin	6 St John's Close		London	SW4 6CV	thegriffins@ntlworld.com	1	No	Yes	Yes
6	Mr	George	Langley	17 Redwing Ave		London	SW3 2KB	georgeLangley231@hot.ail.com	1	No	No	No
7	Miss	Wanda	Patten	21 Long St		London	SW4 7RF	wanda222@hotmail.co.uk	3	No	Yes	Yes
8	Mr	Ken	Souter	Flat 2a	26 Kingsnorth Rd	London	SW5 8GG	kensouter@lineone.net	1	No	Yes	Yes
9	Mr	Brian	Vickers	7 Yalta Rd		London	SW3 7DC	brianFreda@tiscali.com	2	Yes	Yes	No
10	Mrs	Jean	Mendes	5 Fletcher House	Maybush Ave	London	SW4 5SD	jcmendes@hotmail.co.uk	1	Yes	Yes	Yes

Figure 5.10: Questionnaire answers set within a spreadsheet

 Save your spreadsheet as **PotentialCustomers.xls** in the **Analysis** folder.

You will need this spreadsheet for the mail merge in Chapter 11.

Exercise 2: Analysing data

Perform an analysis on the data you have collected in the spreadsheet to find, for example, the percentage of people who:

- have at least one PC at home
- currently own a flash memory stick
- would be interested in a PC healthcheck service.

Good Marks... ✓

You will get good marks if you:

- collect useful information from secondary sources

- contact potential customers to find out what they think

- record the results of your research in a format that is easy to analyse

- analyse your potential customers' responses

- keep your potential customers' contact details for marketing purposes

- keep a project diary of your day-to-day tasks

- keep evidence of your contribution to the work of the group in collecting and analysing data.

Bad Marks... ✗

You will lose marks if you:

- do not have a group meeting to decide on each individual's contribution

- do not keep your plan up-to-date with any changes.

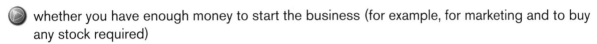

Chapter 6 – Financial planning

Financing the business

Once you have come up with a business idea you need to work out some figures. For example, you need to work out:

- whether you have enough money to start the business (for example, for marketing and to buy any stock required)

- whether the business will make a profit

- what the financial risks are (for example, how much money you might lose if things don't work out as expected).

It will be useful to create a **budget** and a **cash flow statement** for your first year of operation.

Using spreadsheet models

The best tool to help you with this is a spreadsheet. In this chapter you will build a spreadsheet model which will help you to decide:

- how much capital you need in order to start your business

- how much you need to charge for your products and services

- how much you need to sell in order to break even.

The great advantage of using a spreadsheet is that you can alter, for example, the number of items you expect to sell, and see what effect that has on profits.

You would like to be able to show potential investors that even if the business gets off to a slow start, it will soon start making a profit!

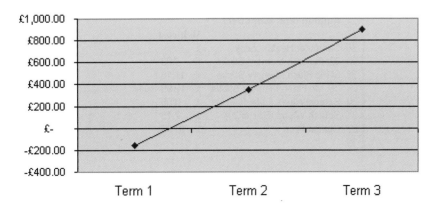

Figure 6.1: Example profit chart

Chapter 6 – Financial planning

Planning the budget

We will assume that you will only operate in term-time, selling hardware items and servicing computers. So you will need to work out figures for three terms, which could be: January–April, May–July and September–December.

Assume for the purpose of this task that you are offering a basic computer healthcheck and you are also hoping to sell flash memory sticks of 32Mb, 64Mb and 256Mb capacities, screen wipes and optical mice.

You have looked up prices on the Internet and made a note of the best deals you can find.

▶ Load **Excel**, and you should see a blank worksheet on your screen.

▶ Enter the following labels and numbers into the spreadsheet.

	A	B	C
1	Colin's Computer Clinic		
2	**Budget**		
3			
4	**Spring term (Jan-Apr)**		
5		Unit cost	
6	Computer Health-check	£ -	
7	32Mb Flash Memory Sticks	£ 4.00	
8	64Mb Flash Memory Sticks	£ 11.16	
9	256Mb Flash Memory Sticks	£ 12.99	
10	Screen Wipes (individual)	£ 0.06	
11	Screen Wipes (Box of 20)	£ 2.13	
12	Optical Mice	£ 16.99	
13			
14	**Summer term (May-Jul)**		
15		Unit cost	
16	Computer Health-check	£ -	
17	32Mb Flash Memory Sticks	£ 4.00	
18	64Mb Flash Memory Sticks	£ 11.16	
19	256Mb Flash Memory Sticks	£ 12.99	
20	Screen Wipes (individual)	£ 0.06	
21	Screen Wipes (Box of 20)	£ 2.13	
22	Optical Mice	£ 16.99	
23			
24	**Autumn term (Sept-Dec)**		
25		Unit cost	
26	Computer Health-check	£ -	
27	32Mb Flash Memory Sticks	£ 4.00	
28	64Mb Flash Memory Sticks	£ 11.16	
29	256Mb Flash Memory Sticks	£ 12.99	
30	Screen Wipes (individual)	£ 0.06	
31	Screen Wipes (Box of 20)	£ 2.13	
32	Optical Mice	£ 16.99	
33			

Figure 6.2: Starting the budget

Deciding on purchase quantities

Businesses often make their profit by purchasing in large quantities at a discount then selling individual items for a higher price. There is a trade-off here – if you buy a large quantity you may get a higher discount but you may also have to borrow money to pay for the goods and you could get stuck with them if you cannot sell them.

You have to estimate how many you think you can sell in three months, or even a year, and do some research to find the best deal you can get.

 Enter the following estimated sales quantities for the first term. The figure in cell D13 is a formula **=SUM(D7:D12)**.

4	Spring term (Jan-Apr)			
5		Unit cost	Purchase Qty	Total Cost
6	Computer Health-check	£ -		
7	32Mb Flash Memory Sticks	£ 4.00	100	£ 400.00
8	64Mb Flash Memory Sticks	£ 11.16	20	£ 223.20
9	256Mb Flash Memory Sticks	£ 12.99	5	£ 64.95
10	Screen Wipes (individual)	£ 0.06	100	£ 6.00
11	Screen Wipes (Box of 20)	£ 2.13	3	£ 6.39
12	Optical Mice	£ 16.99	3	£ 50.97
13				£ 751.51

Figure 6.3: Estimating sales quantities

Calculating gross profit

Next you have to decide how much you are going to charge for each item. The beauty of a spreadsheet is that you can easily change any of the figures if your calculations show that you will not make a profit.

 Enter the following figures in columns E–G. Make sure you enter a formula in cell G13.

4	Spring term (Jan-Apr)						
5		Unit cost	Purchase Qty	Total Cost	Sales Qty	Unit Price	Total Sales
6	Computer Health-check	£ -			12	£ 10.00	£ 120.00
7	32Mb Flash Memory Sticks	£ 4.00	100	£ 400.00	30	£ 8.00	£ 240.00
8	64Mb Flash Memory Sticks	£ 11.16	20	£ 223.20	15	£ 15.00	£ 225.00
9	256Mb Flash Memory Sticks	£ 12.99	5	£ 64.95	5	£ 25.00	£ 125.00
10	Screen Wipes (individual)	£ 0.06	100	£ 6.00	30	£ 0.20	£ 6.00
11	Screen Wipes (Box of 20)	£ 2.13	3	£ 6.39	3	£ 3.50	£ 10.50
12	Optical Mice	£ 16.99	3	£ 50.97	3	£ 20.00	£ 60.00
13				£ 751.51			£ 786.50

Figure 6.4: Calculating the total sales value

Now you can fill in some figures for the next two terms.

▶ Enter the following figures, using formulae for the totals.

	A	B	C	D	E	F	G
1	Colin's Computer Clinic						
2	**Budget**						
3							
4	**Spring term (Jan-Apr)**						
5		Unit cost	Purchase Qty	Total Cost	Sales Qty	Unit Price	Total Sales
6	Computer Health-check	£ -			12	£ 10.00	£ 120.00
7	32Mb Flash Memory Sticks	£ 4.00	100	£ 400.00	30	£ 8.00	£ 240.00
8	64Mb Flash Memory Sticks	£ 11.16	20	£ 223.20	15	£ 15.00	£ 225.00
9	256Mb Flash Memory Sticks	£ 12.99	5	£ 64.95	5	£ 25.00	£ 125.00
10	Screen Wipes (individual)	£ 0.06	100	£ 6.00	30	£ 0.20	£ 6.00
11	Screen Wipes (Box of 20)	£ 2.13	3	£ 6.39	3	£ 3.50	£ 10.50
12	Optical Mice	£ 16.99	3	£ 50.97	3	£ 20.00	£ 60.00
13				£ 751.51			£ 786.50
14	**Summer term (May-Jul)**						
15		Unit cost	Purchase Qty	Total Cost	Sales Qty	Unit Price	Total Sales
16	Computer Health-check	£ -			12	£ 10.00	£ 120.00
17	32Mb Flash Memory Sticks	£ 4.00	0	£ -	30	£ 8.00	£ 240.00
18	64Mb Flash Memory Sticks	£ 11.16	10	£ 111.60	15	£ 15.00	£ 225.00
19	256Mb Flash Memory Sticks	£ 12.99	5	£ 64.95	5	£ 25.00	£ 125.00
20	Screen Wipes (individual)	£ 0.06	0	£ -	30	£ 0.20	£ 6.00
21	Screen Wipes (Box of 20)	£ 2.13	3	£ 6.39	3	£ 3.50	£ 10.50
22	Optical Mice	£ 16.99	3	£ 50.97	3	£ 20.00	£ 60.00
23				£ 233.91			£ 786.50
24	**Autumn term (Sept-Dec)**						
25		Unit cost	Purchase Qty	Total Cost	Sales Qty	Unit Price	Total Sales
26	Computer Health-check	£ -			12	£ 10.00	£ 120.00
27	32Mb Flash Memory Sticks	£ 4.00	0	£ -	40	£ 8.00	£ 320.00
28	64Mb Flash Memory Sticks	£ 11.16	20	£ 223.20	20	£ 15.00	£ 300.00
29	256Mb Flash Memory Sticks	£ 12.99	6	£ 77.94	6	£ 25.00	£ 150.00
30	Screen Wipes (individual)	£ 0.06	0	£ -	30	£ 0.20	£ 6.00
31	Screen Wipes (Box of 20)	£ 2.13	3	£ 6.39	3	£ 3.50	£ 10.50
32	Optical Mice	£ 16.99	3	£ 50.97	5	£ 20.00	£ 100.00
33				£ 358.50			£ 1,006.50

Figure 6.5: Figures for year 1

Smartening up the spreadsheet

You can improve the appearance of your spreadsheet by using various presentation and formatting features. We will insert some blank lines, merge some of the cells and add some colors and shading.

▶ Select cells A1 to G1 and click the **Merge and Center** button.

▶ Enlarge the text and use the **Fill Color** button to shade it blue (or a colour of your own choice).

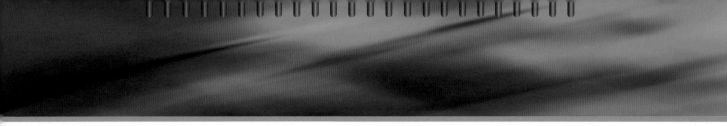

● **Merge and center** the cells in Row 2, and format the text to make it larger, bold and coloured.

● Select and right-click the row headers for Rows 3–5 and select **Insert** to insert three new rows.

● Continue formatting text and inserting new rows to make your spreadsheet look like the one below.

	A	B	C	D	E	F	G
1				Colin's Computer Clinic			
2				Budget			
3							
4							
5							
6							
7	**Spring term (Jan-Apr)**						
8		Unit cost	Purchase Qty	Total Cost	Sales Qty	Unit Price	Total Sales
9	Computer Health-check	£ -			12	£ 10.00	£ 120.00
10	32Mb Flash Memory Sticks	£ 4.00	100	£ 400.00	30	£ 8.00	£ 240.00
11	64Mb Flash Memory Sticks	£ 11.16	20	£ 223.20	15	£ 15.00	£ 225.00
12	256Mb Flash Memory Sticks	£ 12.99	5	£ 64.95	5	£ 25.00	£ 125.00
13	Screen Wipes (individual)	£ 0.06	100	£ 6.00	30	£ 0.20	£ 6.00
14	Screen Wipes (Box of 20)	£ 2.13	3	£ 6.39	3	£ 3.50	£ 10.50
15	Optical Mice	£ 16.99	3	£ 50.97	3	£ 20.00	£ 60.00
16				£ 751.51			£ 786.50
17							
18	**Summer term (May-Jul)**						
19		Unit cost	Purchase Qty	Total Cost	Sales Qty	Unit Price	Total Sales
20	Computer Health-check	£ -			12	£ 10.00	£ 120.00
21	32Mb Flash Memory Sticks	£ 4.00	0	£ -	30	£ 8.00	£ 240.00
22	64Mb Flash Memory Sticks	£ 11.16	10	£ 111.60	15	£ 15.00	£ 225.00
23	256Mb Flash Memory Sticks	£ 12.99	5	£ 64.95	5	£ 25.00	£ 125.00
24	Screen Wipes (individual)	£ 0.06	0	£ -	30	£ 0.20	£ 6.00
25	Screen Wipes (Box of 20)	£ 2.13	3	£ 6.39	3	£ 3.50	£ 10.50
26	Optical Mice	£ 16.99	3	£ 50.97	3	£ 20.00	£ 60.00
27				£ 233.91			£ 786.50
28							
29	**Autumn term (Sept-Dec)**						
30		Unit cost	Purchase Qty	Total Cost	Sales Qty	Unit Price	Total Sales
31	Computer Health-check	£ -			12	£ 10.00	£ 120.00
32	32Mb Flash Memory Sticks	£ 4.00	0	£ -	40	£ 8.00	£ 320.00
33	64Mb Flash Memory Sticks	£ 11.16	20	£ 223.20	20	£ 15.00	£ 300.00
34	256Mb Flash Memory Sticks	£ 12.99	6	£ 77.94	6	£ 25.00	£ 150.00
35	Screen Wipes (individual)	£ 0.06	0	£ -	30	£ 0.20	£ 6.00
36	Screen Wipes (Box of 20)	£ 2.13	3	£ 6.39	3	£ 3.50	£ 10.50
37	Optical Mice	£ 16.99	3	£ 50.97	5	£ 20.00	£ 100.00
38				£ 358.50			£ 1,006.50

Figure 6.6: The formatted spreadsheet

● Save your spreadsheet as **CashFlowForecastv1** in the **Analysis** folder. The next time you save, you could use a different version number (**CashFlowForecastv2**, for example), so that you can show how your spreadsheet developed.

Initial set-up costs

Looking at the figures that you have entered, you will need at least £751.51 to start the business. You will have other expenses as well, for example, you may decide to create a website to advertise your services and to pay an ISP (Internet Service Provider) for website space. Maybe you will also need to buy a bicycle to travel between customers and home, in order to do the computer servicing. Finally, you may need to pay to have your posters and flyers printed.

Cash flow statement

Once you have jotted down all your set-up charges and ongoing expenses, you can draw up a cash flow statement. This shows how much cash you will have available at any given time, if your sales predictions are accurate.

Enter the following cash flow statement below the rest of the figures you have already entered. The screenshot below shows the formulae you should enter. To toggle **Formula view**, select **Tools, Options, View Formula**.

		Cash Flow Statement		
40				
41				
42		**Term 1**	**Term 2**	**Term 3**
43	**Cash out**			
44	Cost of stock	=$D$15	=D26	=D37
45	Marketing costs	50		50
46	Purchase of bike	100		
47	ISP charges	45	45	45
48	Loan repayment	0	500	500
49	**Total cash out**	=SUM(B44:B48)	=SUM(C44:C48)	=SUM(D44:D48)
50				
51	**Cash in**			
52	Sales	=G15	=G26	=G37
53	Net cash flow (cash in -cash out)	=B52-B49	=C52-C49	=D52-D49
54				
55	Opening balance	1000	=B57	=C57
56	Plus or minus net cash flow	=B53	=C53	=D53
57	**Closing bank balance**	=B55+B56	=C55+C56	=D55+D56

Figure 6.7: The cash flow statement in Formula view

Your cash flow statement should look like Figure 6.8 below.

	A	B	C	D
39				
40	**Cash Flow Statement**			
41				
42		**Term 1**	**Term 2**	**Term 3**
43	**Cash out**			
44	Cost of stock	£ 751.51	£ 233.91	£ 358.50
45	Marketing costs	£ 50.00		£ 50.00
46	Purchase of bike	£ 100.00		
47	ISP charges	£ 45.00	£ 45.00	£ 45.00
48	Loan repayment	£ -	£ 500.00	£ 500.00
49	**Total cash out**	£ 946.51	£ 778.91	£ 953.50
50				
51	**Cash in**			
52	Sales	£ 786.50	£ 786.50	£1,006.50
53	Net cash flow (cash in -cash out)	-£ 160.01	£ 7.59	£ 53.00
54				
55	Opening balance	£ 1,000.00	£ 839.99	£ 847.58
56	Plus or minus net cash flow	-£ 160.01	£ 7.59	£ 53.00
57	**Closing bank balance**	£ 839.99	£ 847.58	£ 900.58

Figure 6.8: A cash flow statement

So far, so good! Your cash flow statement shows that after a year of operation, if all goes according to plan, you will have £900.50 in the bank even after repaying the interest-free loan of £1,000 that you managed to negotiate.

Conditional formatting

You can apply conditional formatting to cells B44 to D47, so that if any of the numbers are negative, they will be displayed in red. To do this:

▶ Select cells B44 to D57, and from the **Format** menu choose **Conditional Formatting**.

The following dialogue box is displayed.

Figure 6.9: Conditional Formatting dialogue box

▶ Set **Condition 1** to **Cell Value is less than 0** and then press the **Format** button.

▶ Set the font colour to **red** and click **OK**. The new conditional format will be displayed. Click **OK** to set the format.

Any cells with negative values should now be displayed in red.

Profit and loss statement

You started off with no money of your own, so you will have made a profit of £900.50. You can show this in a profit and loss statement, which shows basically the same figures in a slightly different format.

⊙ Enter the labels, figures and formulae for the profit and loss statement, starting in cell H40.

	H	I	J	K
40	**Profit and Loss Statement**			
41				
42		**Term 1**	**Term 2**	**Term 3**
43	Cash out			
44	Cost of stock	=$D$16	=D27	=D38
45	Marketing costs	50		50
46	Purchase of bike	100		
47	ISP charges	45	45	45
48				
49	Total cash out	=SUM(I44:I48)	=SUM(J44:J48)	=SUM(K44:K48)
50				
51	Cash in			
52	Sales	=G16	=G27	=G38
53	Profit	=I52-I49	=J52-J49	=K52-K49
54				
55				
56				
57	Cumulative profit	=I53	=I57+J53	=J57+K53

Figure 6.10: A profit and loss statement in Formula view

Your profit and loss statement should look like this:

	H	I	J	K
40	**Profit and Loss Statement**			
41				
42		**Term 1**	**Term 2**	**Term 3**
43	**Cash out**			
44	Cost of stock	£ 751.51	£ 233.91	£ 358.50
45	Marketing costs	£ 50.00		£ 50.00
46	Purchase of bike	£ 100.00		
47	ISP charges	£ 45.00	£ 45.00	£ 45.00
48				
49	**Total cash out**	£ 946.51	£ 278.91	£ 453.50
50				
51	**Cash in**			
52	Sales	£ 786.50	£ 786.50	£1,006.50
53	Profit	-£ 160.01	£ 507.59	£ 553.00
54				
55				
56				
57	**Cumulative profit**	-£ 160.01	£ 347.58	£ 900.58

Figure 6.11: A profit and loss statement

⊙ Save your spreadsheet as **CashFlowForecastv2** in the **Analysis** folder.

Adding a header and footer

It is a good idea to add a header, a footer, or both, to identify the name of your spreadsheet as well as items such as your own name, date created and pathname, so that you can easily find it again on your computer.

▶ From the **View** menu select **Header and Footer**.

▶ In the **Page Setup** dialogue box, click the drop-down arrow in the **Header** box and select the spreadsheet name.

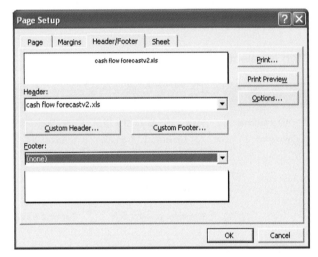

Figure 6.12: Page Setup dialogue box

We will create a custom footer giving the author's name and the date created.

▶ Click the **Custom Footer** button and the **Footer** box appears.

▶ Enter **Created by Colin Blake** in the left-hand box.

▶ With the cursor in the right-hand box, click the **Date** icon.

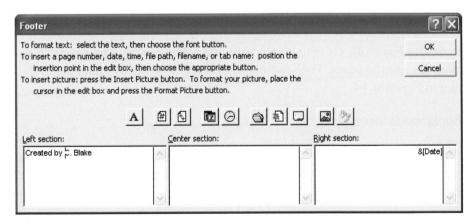

Figure 6.13: Footer box

▶ Adjust the font size if you wish, following the instructions on the screen, and then press **OK**. Press **OK** again to return to your spreadsheet.

▶ Click the **Print Preview** button to see your header and footer.

Displaying formulae

In your final eportfolio, you should include a spreadsheet which shows all the formulae you used. To display the formulae rather than the values follow the steps below.

▶ From the main menu select **Tools**, **Options**.

▶ Make sure the **View** tab is selected and tick the **Formulas** box.

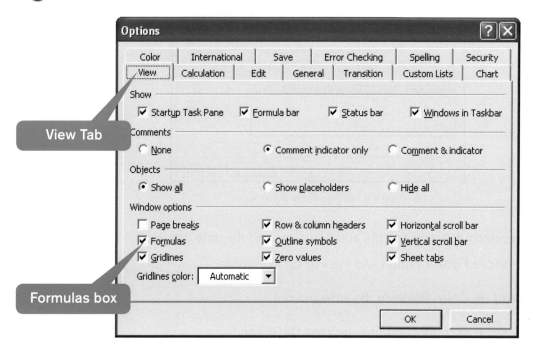

Figure 6.14: Displaying formulae

▶ You can use the **Formula view** to check your spreadsheet formulae against Figure 6.10 if your figures are not the same. Then restore it to **Normal view** by unchecking the **Formulas** box shown in Figure 6.14.

▶ **Save** your spreadsheet again.

In the next chapter you will draw a graph showing profit made over the year. Then you will develop the spreadsheet, using the model to explore the effects of varying the amounts sold and the prices charged.

We will start by drawing a graph showing the cumulative profit from January to December.

▶ Load the spreadsheet **CashFlowForecastv2**.

▶ Select cells H42:K42 containing the headings **Term 1**, **Term 2**, etc. Then keep your finger on the **Ctrl** key while you select H57:K57, containing the figures for profit.

▶ Click the **Chart** icon and select **Line** as the type of chart. Press **Next**.

Chart Icon

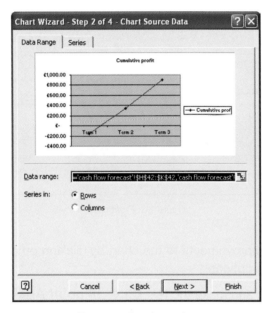

Figure 7.1: Creating a chart

▶ In **Chart Wizard Step 3** (Chart Options), select the **Legend** tab and uncheck **Show legend**. Click **Next**.

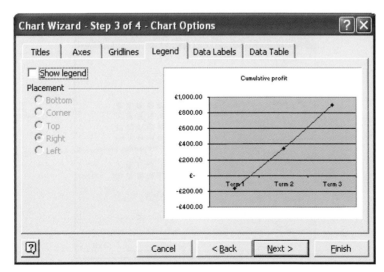

Figure 7.2: Chart Wizard Step 3 of 4

In **Chart Wizard Step 4**, leave the default **Place chart As Object in CashFlowForecastv2**. Click **Finish**.

The chart appears in the spreadsheet. You can drag it so that it does not hide any of your figures.

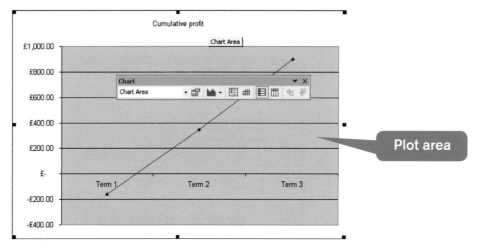

Figure 7.3: Profit chart

You can now make various improvements to the chart by clicking on different parts of it and choosing different formatting options.

Right-click the chart title and make the text **Blue, 14 point Arial**.

Right-click the x-axis and select **Format axis**. Make the data labels **Low**, so that they appear under the chart.

Right-click the plot area and select **Format Plot Area**. In the **Format Plot Area** dialogue box change the colour to something cheerful.

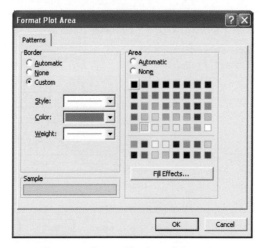

Figure 7.4: Format Plot Area dialogue box

Your chart should now look something like the one shown in Figure 7.5.

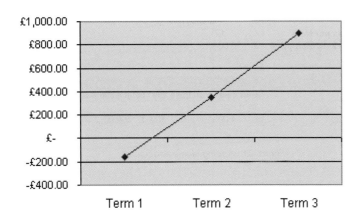

Figure 7.5: The finished chart

 Save your spreadsheet.

Sensitivity analysis

The predicted profit looks impressive. But don't forget that it is just a prediction and involves a large amount of guesswork. If your forecast turns out to be unrealistic, it is probably because:

- your expectations were unrealistic

- your assumptions were not objective

- you did not have enough information to make accurate predictions.

Using your spreadsheet you can carry out a **sensitivity analysis** to see how much difference it will make to your profit if you adjust some of the figures. Your predictions show that you will make a lot of profit on the computer healthchecks, which cost you nothing. You have also assumed that you can buy 32Mb flash memory sticks at £4.00 and sell them at £8.00. But what if nobody buy's them at that price? You will then have to reduce the cost.

We will perform the sensitivity analysis on these two items: the number of computer healthchecks and the selling price of the 32Mb Flash memory sticks.

One way to do this is to hold these two figures separately and use an absolute cell reference to refer to them wherever they occur in the spreadsheet. You can then try out different figures to see how the profit is affected.

⊙ Enter the labels and figures in rows 4 and 5 as shown in Figure 7.6 below.

	A	B	C	D	E	F	G
1	Colin's Computer Clinic						
2	Budget						
3	Number of health-checks per term	12					
4	32Mb Flash memory sticks selling price	£ 8.00					
5							
6							
7	Spring term (Jan-Apr)						
8		Unit cost	Purchase Qty	Total Cost	Sales Qty	Unit Price	Total Sales
9	Computer Health-check	£ -			12	£ 10.00	£ 120.00
10	32Mb Flash Memory Sticks	£ 4.00	100	£ 400.00	30	£ 8.00	£ 240.00

Figure 7.6: Adding labels and figures

We will name cells B4 and B5 so that we can use the names as absolute references.

⊙ Select cell B4. Click in the **Name Box** and type the name **Healthchecks**. Then press **Enter**.

Healthchecks ▼   ƒx 8

	A	B	C	D	E	F	G
1	Colin's Computer Clinic						
2	Budget						
3	Number of health-checks per term	12					
4	32Mb Flash memory sticks selling price	£ 8.00					
5							
6							
7	Spring term (Jan-Apr)						
8		Unit cost	Purchase Qty	Total Cost	Sales Qty	Unit Price	Total Sales
9	Computer Health-check	£ -			12	£ 10.00	£ 120.00
10	32Mb Flash Memory Sticks	£ 4.00	100	£ 400.00	30	£ 8.00	£ 240.00

Figure 7.7: Naming a cell

⊙ Select cell B5. Click in the **Name Box** and type the name **Flash32**. Then press **Enter**.

⊙ Select cell E9 and type the formula **=Healthchecks**.

⊙ **Copy** this cell to cells E20 and E31.

⊙ Replace cell F10 with the formula **=Flash32**.

⊙ **Copy** this cell to cells F21 and F32.

Now you are ready to try out some different forecasts. For example;

- What if you only do four healthchecks per term?

- What if you are forced to sell the 32Mb flash memory sticks for £6.00?

Your profit is reduced to £460.58.

▶ Try some other variations. Notice how the cumulative profit chart automatically adjusts when you change the figures.

▶ You can test out the effect of altering some of the other figures too, for example, the quantity of flash memory sticks that you think you will sell.

Break-even analysis

A break-even analysis will show you how much you absolutely must sell, in various combinations, in order to break even.

▶ Try altering the quantities of each type of flash memory stick sold in each term until your final profit figure in cell K57 is approximately zero.

▶ Save the spreadsheet as **CashflowForecastv3** in the **Analysis** folder.

	A	B	C	D	E	F	G	H	I	J	K
1	Colin's Computer Clinic										
2	Budget										
3	Number of health-checks per term	12									
4	32Mb Flash memory sticks selling price	£ 8.00									
5											
6											
7	Spring term (Jan-Apr)										
8			Unit cost	Purchase Qty	Total Cos	Sales Qty	Unit Price	Total Sales			
9	Computer Health-check	£ -			4	£ 10.00	£ 40.00				
10	32Mb Flash Memory Sticks	£ 4.00	100	£ 400.00	5	£ 6.00	£ 30.00				
11	64Mb Flash Memory Sticks	£ 11.16	20	£ 223.20	15	£ 15.00	£ 225.00				
12	256Mb Flash Memory Sticks	£ 12.99	5	£ 64.95	5	£ 25.00	£ 125.00				
13	Screen Wipes (individual)	£ 0.06	100	£ 6.00	30	£ 0.20	£ 6.00				
14	Screen Wipes (Box of 20)	£ 2.13	3	£ 6.39	3	£ 3.50	£ 10.50				
15	Optical Mice	£ 16.99	3	£ 50.97	3	£ 20.00	£ 60.00				
16					£ 751.51			£ 496.50			
17											
18	Summer term (May-Jul)										
19			Unit cost	Purchase Qty	Total Cos	Sales Qty	Unit Price	Total Sales			
20	Computer Health-check	£ -			4	£ 10.00	£ 40.00				
21	32Mb Flash Memory Sticks	£ 4.00	0	£ -	8	£ 6.00	£ 48.00				
22	64Mb Flash Memory Sticks	£ 11.16	10	£ 111.60	15	£ 15.00	£ 225.00				
23	256Mb Flash Memory Sticks	£ 12.99	5	£ 64.95	5	£ 25.00	£ 125.00				
24	Screen Wipes (individual)	£ 0.06	0	£ -	30	£ 0.20	£ 6.00				
25	Screen Wipes (Box of 20)	£ 2.13	3	£ 6.39	3	£ 3.50	£ 10.50				
26	Optical Mice	£ 16.99	3	£ 50.97	3	£ 20.00	£ 60.00				
27					£ 233.91			£ 514.50			
28											
29	Autumn term (Sept-Dec)										
30			Unit cost	Purchase Qty	Total Cos	Sales Qty	Unit Price	Total Sales			
31	Computer Health-check	£ -			4	£ 10.00	£ 40.00				
32	32Mb Flash Memory Sticks	£ 4.00	0	£ -	10	£ 6.00	£ 60.00				
33	64Mb Flash Memory Sticks	£ 11.16	20	£ 223.20	20	£ 15.00	£ 300.00				
34	256Mb Flash Memory Sticks	£ 12.99	6	£ 77.94	6	£ 25.00	£ 150.00				
35	Screen Wipes (individual)	£ 0.06	0	£ -	30	£ 0.20	£ 6.00				
36	Screen Wipes (Box of 20)	£ 2.13	3	£ 6.39	3	£ 3.50	£ 10.50				
37	Optical Mice	£ 16.99	3	£ 50.97	5	£ 20.00	£ 100.00				
38					£ 358.50			£ 666.50			
39											
40	Cash Flow Statement							Profit and Loss Statement			
41											
42			Term 1	Term 2	Term 3				Term 1	Term 2	Term 3
43	Cash out							Cash out			
44	Cost of stock		£ 751.51	£ 233.91	£ 358.50			Cost of stock	£ 751.51	£ 233.91	£ 358.50
45	Marketing costs		£ 50.00		£ 50.00			Marketing costs	£ 50.00		£ 50.00
46	Purchase of bike		£ 100.00					Purchase of bike	£ 100.00		
47	ISP charges		£ 45.00	£ 45.00	£ 45.00			ISP charges	£ 45.00	£ 45.00	£ 45.00
48	Loan repayment		£ -	£ 500.00	£ 500.00						
49	Total cash out		£ 946.51	£ 778.91	£ 953.50			Total cash out	£ 946.51	£ 278.91	£ 453.50
50											
51	Cash in							Cash in			
52	Sales		£ 496.50	£ 514.50	£ 666.50			Sales	£ 496.50	£ 514.50	£ 666.50
53	Net cash flow (cash in - cash out)		-£ 450.01	-£ 264.41	-£ 287.00			Profit	-£ 450.01	£ 235.59	£ 213.00
54											
55	Opening balance		£ 1,000.00	£ 549.99	£ 285.58						
56	Plus or minus net cash flow		-£ 450.01	-£ 264.41	-£ 287.00						
57	Closing bank balance		£ 549.99	£ 285.58	-£ 1.42			Cumulative profit	-£ 450.01	-£ 214.42	-£ 1.42

Figure 7.8: CashflowForecastv3

Chapter 7 – Financial anaylsis

Good Marks... ✓

You will get good marks if you:

- collect suitable data to put in your spreadsheet

- create a cash flow forecast and break-even analysis

- use a chart or graph to show the predicted profit

- calculate 'what if' scenarios to show the effects of changing sales quantities, cost prices and/or sales prices

- have kept your project diary and plan up-to-date.

Bad Marks... ✗

You will lose marks if you:

- use unrealistic figures

- have mistakes in your formulae or calculations

- do not lay out the spreadsheet so that it is easy to understand

- do not show the break-even analysis and 'what if' analysis.

The importance of a corporate identity

All businesses need a corporate identity so that their customers can instantly recognise who they are and what they do when they see their logos or slogans.

Getting the logo and slogan right can be very beneficial and some companies such as British Telecom and the Royal Mail will spend millions researching and designing a new name and logo.

Designing a new logo

A new logo will often relate to the nature of the business in some way. This helps people who do not already recognise the logo to guess the type of company that it belongs to. However, some companies such as McDonalds, Nike and Coca Cola have logos that on their own carry no indication of the nature of the company. We all know what they do, though, because of their marketing. You could also try to incorporate the company name or initials into the logo.

A good logo will work in large and small sizes, monochrome, in different colours and on different backgrounds.

You should use an art or graphics software package such as **Adobe Photoshop Elements** to create the logo. You will then be able to import the image file into any document you want. Designing it in **Word**, for example, can make it difficult to export to other programs.

 Tip:

Try roughing out several ideas or using a Mind Map to assemble your thoughts on a piece of paper before getting stuck in. You could also try looking at some logos from other companies on the Internet for ideas. Write down all of the attributes of your company that you want to portray, such as modern, rustic, eco-friendly, healthy or helpful, for example. Choose styles and colours that help to reflect these. Remember, the simplest designs are often the most effective.

Choosing a colour scheme

Once you have a few ideas for your logo, you need to decide on an appropriate colour scheme. For some companies this really matters but for others it makes little difference. The BP logo above (second from left) is mostly green which is very distinctive within the oil industry and it helps convey a positive brand image for the company.

The colour scheme that you choose for the logo will become the major colour scheme for all of your stationery, your website and the overall company image, so it is important that you start off with something that you are satisfied with.

You can try putting blocks of colour next to each other to test out how they look together, as shown below.

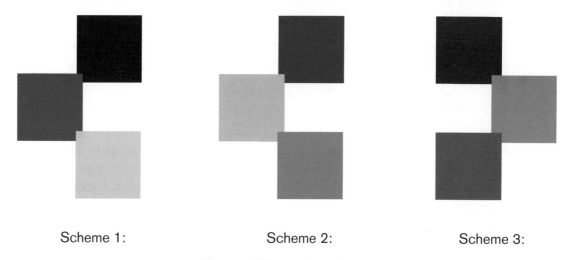

Scheme 1:   Scheme 2:   Scheme 3:

Figure 8.1: Different colour schemes

Keep each of your colour schemes apart to make it easier to judge which you like the best.

Getting feedback

You should try showing your colour schemes and any logo ideas to friends and relatives, and find out what their opinion is. They may have some very useful feedback. Having shown these schemes to people, the general feedback was that the second scheme 'looked a little more computery'.

It is important to continue getting feedback as your logo develops in order to end up with the best possible image. You should show evidence of any development in your eportfolio at the end of the project.

Developing Colin's logo using Photoshop Elements

Although this will be a very simple logo, it still uses several of the basic functions of **Photoshop Elements**.

▶ Open **Adobe Photoshop Elements 2.0**.

▶ Click **New File** on the opening window.

Setting the resolution correctly

The resolution of an image is the number of dots or pixels per square inch. The more pixels there are, the sharper the image will be. For images that are going to be seen only on-screen, 72 pixels per inch is fine, but for anything that will be printed you should set the resolution to at least 300 pixels per inch. Since this logo will be printed on stationery it is important to use 300 pixels per inch.

- In the **New** document dialogue box, set the **Width** and **Height** to **6 cm**.

- Change the **Resolution** to **300 pixels/inch**.

- Set the **Contents** to **Transparent**. This will give your logo a transparent background so that you will later be able to use it on other backgrounds without it having a white border.

Figure 8.2: Image settings

- Click **OK**. Your screen should now look like Figure 8.3, with the toolbar on the left.

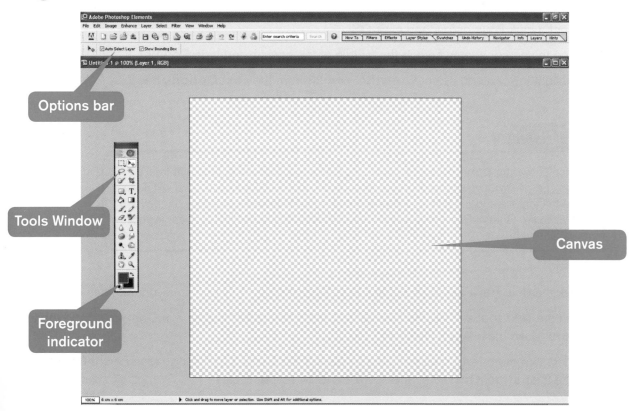

Figure 8.3: Photoshop Elements main screen

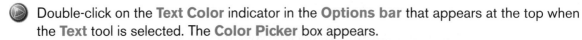

T.

Text tool

● Click on the **Text** tool in the **Tools** window.

● Double-click on the **Text Color** indicator in the **Options bar** that appears at the top when the **Text** tool is selected. The **Color Picker** box appears.

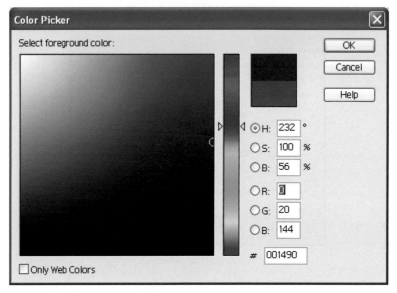

Figure 8.4: The Color Picker box

● Select a dark **Blue** colour and click **OK**.

● Place the cursor somewhere in the middle of the canvas and type **Colin's**.

● Highlight the text and select **Outwrite**, size **24** from the **Text Options** bar.

 Tip:

If you don't have the **Outwrite** font in your fonts list, you can download the font from **www.payne-gallway.co.uk**; click on the relevant link in the DiDA section. You will need to unzip the font file and put it in your **Fonts** folder in the **Windows** directory on the hard drive (within the Control Panel on your computer). It should automatically appear in your fonts list after this.

● Click the **tick mark** at the end of the **Text Options** bar. This confirms your choices so far.

● With the **Text** tool still selected create two more text boxes and type in **Computer** and then **Clinic**. Make them **Blue**, **Outwrite**, size **24**.

● Create two more text boxes to hold a single capital **C** and **3** of the logo (see Figure 8.5). Make them **Blue**, **Outwrite**, and size **72** and **24** respectively.

Moving objects around the canvas

 Select the **Move** tool in the top-right of the **Tools** window.

 Rearrange the five text boxes so that they appear as shown in Figure 8.5.

Move tool

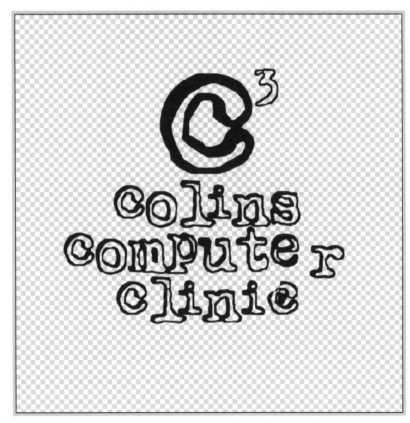

Figure 8.5: Example logo

Understanding layers

Each text box that you have put on the canvas belongs to a different layer in the overall image. Imagine that every piece of text is written on a separate piece of see-through plastic, all stacked on top of each other. If you want to shade a particular piece of text you need to do it on that particular layer.

 Select **Window**, **Layers** from the main menu. You will see a box similar to that shown in Figure 8.6.

 You can move layers up and down the 'stack' by dragging them around in the **Layers** panel.

 With the **Move** tool selected, try clicking on each of the layers in the palette and see which parts of the main image become active.

Move tool

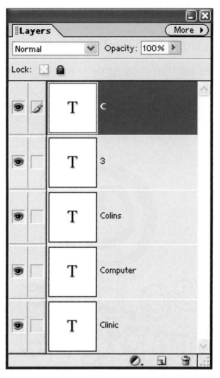

Figure 8.6: The Layers panel

Shading the text

At the moment, **Photoshop** sees the text as regular text, so you can still change the font and edit it. If you want to colour it, you need to tell **Photoshop** to convert the text to a regular bitmap image. This means that you will no longer to be able to edit it as normal text.

Paint Bucket tool

▶ Select the **Paint Bucket** tool.

▶ Double-click the **Colour Indicator** and select a **Pale Blue**.

▶ Select the layer called **C** in the **Layers** palette.

▶ Click in the large **C** to fill it in with the **Pale Blue**. A warning message will appear.

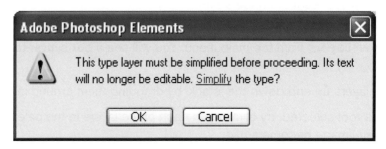

Figure 8.7: Photoshop warning message

Click **OK** to simplify the image and then try to fill it in again. This time it should turn blue.

Click on the layer called **Colin's** and fill in each of the letters in turn using the same blue.

Do the same with the **Computer** and **Clinic** layers. Remember to select the layer you want to work on first!

Now select a bright green from the colour palette and shade in the **3** to make it stand out. Your finished logo should look like the one in Figure 8.8.

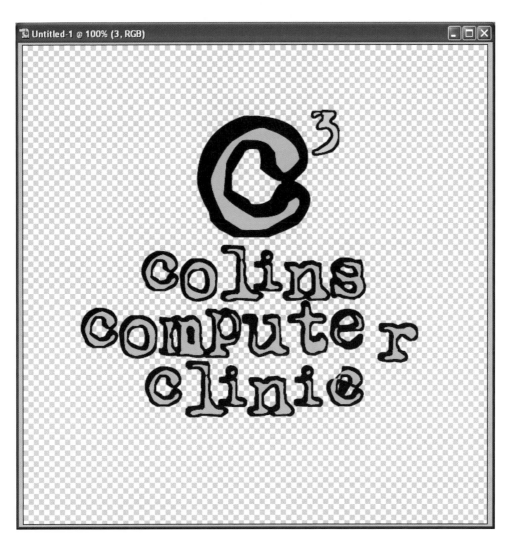

Figure 8.8: Logo with fill colours added

Cropping the excess canvas

Selection tool

▶ Use the **Selection** tool to draw a rectangle around the entire image.

▶ Select **Image**, **Crop** from the main menu to cut off the excess canvas.

The finished logo should look like the one in Figure 8.9.

Figure 8.9: The finished logo

▶ **Save** the image as **Logo.psd**.

Saving an image as another file format

Photoshop will automatically give all of its files the default extension **.psd**. This identifies it to the computer as a **Photoshop** file type. If you want to import it into other documents, you will need to save it as a format that they will recognise easily, such as **.bmp**, **.jpg** or **.gif**.

> **Tip:**
>
> If you have a transparent background and wish to keep it you will need to save it as a **.gif** file.

With the **Logo.psd** file still open in **Photoshop**, select **File**, **Save As** from the main menu.

 In the **Save As** dialogue box, select **CompuServe GIF (*.GIF)** from the **Format** option box.

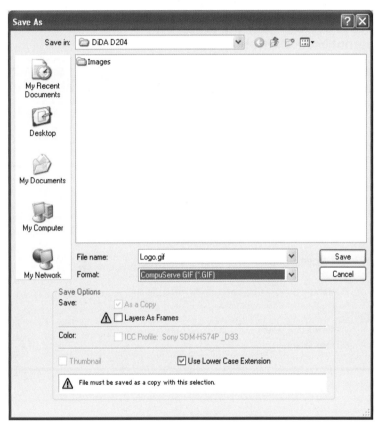

Figure 8.10: Saving an image in GIF format

 Click **Save**.

 Click **OK** in the next window and **OK** again.

Adding a strapline

A strapline is a slogan or very short sentence that in some way advertises your company or one element of it which you want to stress. Some examples of these are Tesco's 'Every little helps' and the National Lottery's 'It could be you…'.

Using a similar method to the way in which you planned your logo, go back to your sheet of ideas and try to put together a few words that help describe exactly what your company is going to do.

Since **Colin's Computer Clinic** is all about preventing viruses and generally increasing the performance and efficiency of your PC, a suitable strapline might be something to do with speed and making life easier.

Creating the strapline

⊚ Open **Photoshop Elements 2.0**.

⊚ In the **New** document dialogue box, set the **Width** to **10cm** and the **Height** to **1cm**. Make sure that the **Resolution** is set to **300 pixels/inch**.

⊚ Select **Transparent** in the **Contents** box.

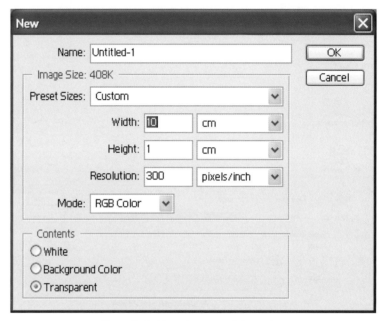

Figure 8.11: New document dialogue box

⊚ Click **OK**.

⊚ Select the **Text** tool from the **Tools** window and type **Putting you back in the fast lane…**

T.

Text tool

⊚ Make the text **Dark Blue**, **Outwrite**, size **14**.

Figure 8.12: Creating a strapline

⊚ In order to emphasise the key word in the phrase, highlight **fast** and make it **Italic**.

Paint Bucket tool

⊚ Using the **Paint Bucket** tool, shade in the text in the same light blue as your logo but make the word **fast** green.

⊡

Selection tool

⊚ Use the **Selection** tool to put a box around the slogan and click **Image**, **Crop** on the main menu to cut off the excess canvas.

The finished strapline image should look like the one in Figure 8.13.

Figure 8.13: The finished strapline image

 Save the file as **Strapline.psd** and again as **Strapline.gif**.

Creating a simplified logo

It would be good to simplify your logo in order to save space on some of your business documents (such as a business card). You could try saving just the **C³** as an image on its own to be used for this.

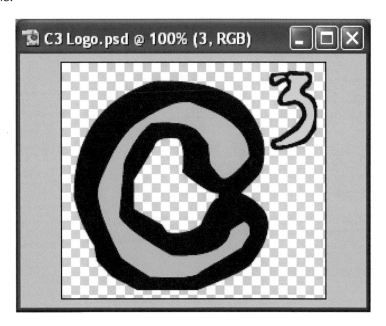

Figure 8.14: A simplified logo

Types of font

There are two main types of font, **sans serif**, which this book uses and **serif** font. Serifs are the pointed ends at each point on a letter. A sample of a serif font is **Times New Roman**. Sans serif means without serifs in French; this text, for example, is written in a sans serif font such as **Ariel**. It is not necessary to use this font for everything but you should include it with a selection of one or two other fonts for the main body text in each document you produce.

Keeping your corporate identity consistent

It is very important that you continue to use these colours and this font in the rest of the marketing and business communications that you produce. People learn to associate different fonts and colour schemes with different companies without even looking at the logo or reading their straplines. Newspapers can be distinguished from one another purely on the fonts they use and some colours on adverts can automatically make you think of particular companies, for example, purple and white – did you think of Cadbury's?

Good Marks... ✓

You will get good marks if you:

- independently produce a possible corporate identity for your group's company

- consider colours, fonts and strapline

- gather feedback on your designs

- modify your designs in response to feedback.

Bad Marks... ✗

You will lose marks if you:

- create your logo in a format which cannot be imported into documents such as posters, flyers, letterheads, etc

- do not update your project diary.

Chapter 9 – Presenting proposals

Now that you have completed your market research and financial analysis, you can present your business plan, based on your research, to potential investors. For example, you could present it to the school's young enterprise committee in order to persuade them to give you the £1000 loan that you need.

Structuring your presentation

It is very important to remember, when creating a pitch like this, exactly who the audience is and what you need to get across.

1. Set the scene.

2. Explain the current situation and highlight the demand for your products or service. Remember that you are trying to sell this service to your investors. If they are convinced of the value of your service, they are more likely to give you the investment that you need.

3. Demonstrate your potential market.

4. Show results from your market research in support of your business.

5. Breakdown the initial investment you need into all the component costs for the investors to see exactly how their money will be spent.

6. Show graphs of potential profits and break-even points or worst-case scenarios. Prove that you have conducted a sensitivity analysis showing the effect on profit of different levels of sales.

7. Give some more ideas for expansion of the business to show that you have also thought of the future.

8. Conclude your presentation.

Creating a PowerPoint presentation

Once you have planned the structure of your presentation, you can start to create it.

- Open **Microsoft PowerPoint**.

- The **Getting Started** window should automatically appear. Click on **Create a new presentation**. If the **Getting Started** window does not appear click on **File**, **New**, to get the **New Presentation** window to appear.

- In the next **New Presentation** dialogue box select **Blank Presentation**.

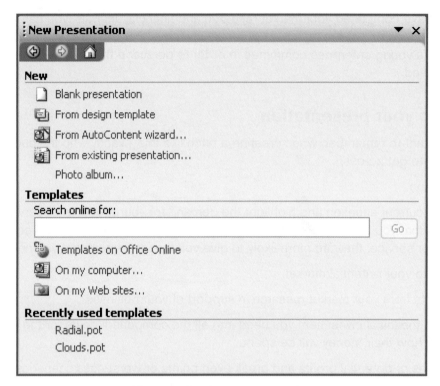

Figure 9.1: Creating a new presentation

In the blank presentation, select the first **Slide Layout** called **Title Slide** and close the **Slide Layout** window.

Using templates and colour schemes

It is possible to automatically set a pre-made template and colour scheme for your presentation using **PowerPoint**.

On the main menu, select **Format**, **Slide Design**.

With the **Design Templates** selected, look through some of the designs that you could choose.

Make sure that you re-select the blank **Default Design** once you have finished looking.

Click the **Color Schemes** option and look at some of the colour schemes that you could choose for your presentation.

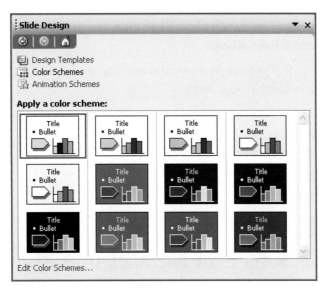

Figure 9.2: Selecting a colour scheme

When you have finished looking, close the **Slide Design** window.

You will not be using a template or pre-made colour scheme for this presentation. Since it is for your company and you have already created the logo, it is best to adopt the logo's colour scheme as your colour scheme throughout this presentation.

Designing your own layout using the Slide Master

Click **View**, **Master**, **Slide Master** on the main menu. The screen now appears as in Figure 9.3.

Figure 9.3: The Slide Master

Rectangle tool

Using the **Rectangle** tool on the **Drawing toolbar**, drag out a narrow box across the top of the slide and shade it **Pale Blue**.

Create another pencil-thin rectangle down the left side and shade this **Bright Green**, to match the colours you used in your logo.

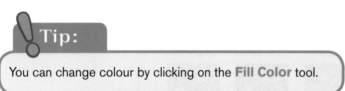

Tip:

You can change colour by clicking on the **Fill Color** tool.

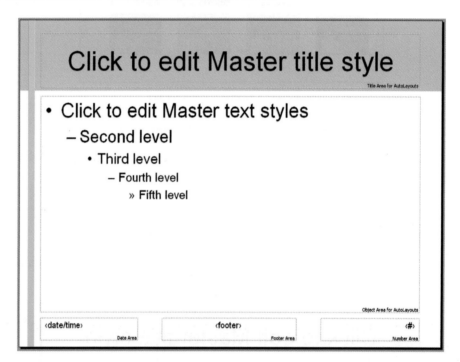

Figure 9.4: Creating a simple custom design

Inserting your logo and strapline images

Click on **Insert**, **Picture From file** on the main menu.

Locate and select the **C3 Logo.gif** file, then resize it to fit in the top right corner of the slide.

Repeat the operation for the **Strapline.gif** image and position this in the bottom right corner.

Resize the **Master title** text box at the top of the slide to fit around the logo.

Delete the **Number Area** and **Footer Area** placeholders behind the strapline image.

The Slide Master should look like the one shown in Figure 9.5.

Figure 9.5: Customised slide design

⏵ **Save** your presentation as **BusinessProposal.ppt**.

⏵ Click on **View, Normal** to exit the **Slide Master View**.

Creating the title slide

Now you can start creating the actual presentation. Every new slide that you create will have the same look as the Slide Master but the first slide will have a different layout from the rest, to emphasise it as the title slide.

⏵ Click to add a title and enter **Colin's**. Press **Enter**.

⏵ Type in **Computer**, press enter again and type **Clinic**.

⏵ Highlight all three words, then, using the **Text Resize** tool, resize the text to size **72**, **Arial** and **Bold**.

⏵ Click the **Left Justify** button.

Text Resize tool

Left Justify button

Adjusting line spacing

⏵ With **Colin's Computer Clinic** highlighted, click **Format, Line Spacing**.

⏵ Enter **0.75** in the **Line Spacing** box and click **OK**.

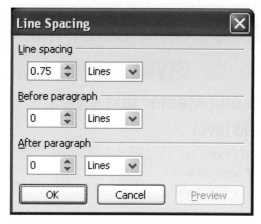

Figure 9.6: Adjusting line spacing

 Enter **Business Proposals** in the **Subtitle** box.

 Make it **Dark Blue** to match the dark blue in the logo.

 Reposition the title and subtitle as shown in Figure 9.7.

Figure 9.7: The first slide

Creating a new slide

 Click the **New Slide** button on the **Formatting** toolbar.

New Slide button

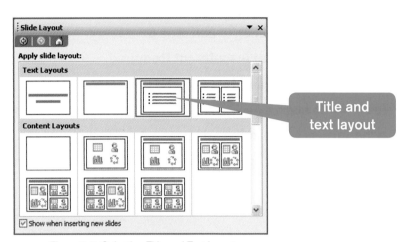

Figure 9.8: Selecting Title and Text layout

Select the **Title and Text** layout and close the **Slide Layout** window.

Enter the text as shown in Figure 9.9.

Complete the following three more slides as shown in Figure 9.9.

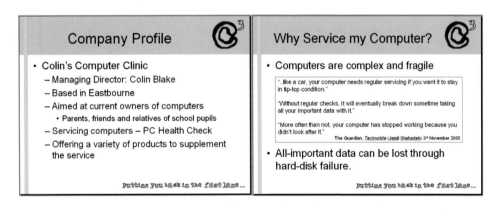

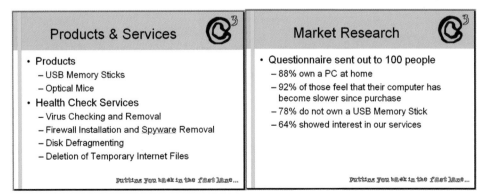

Figure 9.9: Slides 2, 3, 4 and 5

Save what you have done so far.

New Slide button

Bullets button

▶ Click the **New Slide** button to add slide 6.

▶ Enter the heading **Initial Investment Required**.

▶ Begin adding the first line **Start-up loan of £1000**.

▶ Press **Enter** to begin a new line. Click the **Bullets** button to turn bullet points off.

▶ Use the **Tab** key on the keyboard to move the indent in a bit.

▶ Enter the costs as they appear in Figure 9.10. Use the **Tab** key again to keep everything lined up.

Initial Investment Required

• **Start-up loan of £1000**

Cost of Stock	£ 750
Marketing Costs	£ 50
Purchase of Bike	£ 100
ISP Charges	£ 45
Extras	£ 55
Total Investment	£1000

• **Loan to be repaid in 2 instalments of £500 at the end of Term 2 and Term 3.**

putting you back in the fast lane...

Figure 9.10: Slide 6

▶ Reduce the **Font Size** to **20** and colour it **Dark Blue** to make it stand out.

▶ Finish off the rest of the slide as shown in Figure 9.10.

Importing graphs from Microsoft Excel

In slides 7 and 8 you will need to show some financial graphs from the spreadsheet that you created earlier in the book.

▶ Load **Microsoft Excel** alongside your **PowerPoint** presentation.

▶ Open the latest **CashFlowForecast** file.

- Make sure that the **Number of Health Checks per Term** is set to **12** and that the **Selling Price of 32Mb Flash Drives** is set to **£8.00**. The graph should display the potential profits with this combination.

- Select the graph and click **Copy**.

- Return to **PowerPoint** and create a new slide.

- **Paste** the graph into the space on slide 7.

- Add the text shown in Figure 9.11 and resize the graph as necessary.

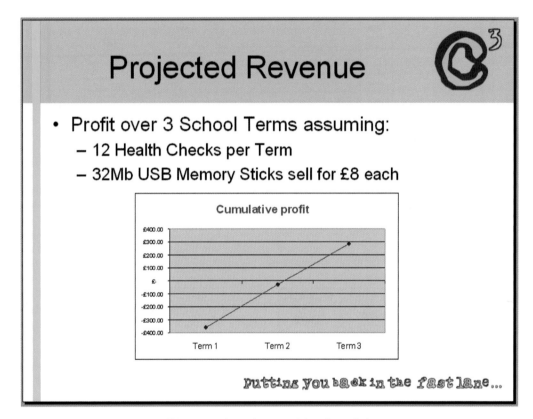

Figure 9.11: Importing a graph into PowerPoint

- Create slide 8 in the same way, making sure that you set the **Number of Health Checks per Term** to **4** and that the **Selling Price of 32Mb Flash memory sticks** is lowered to **£6.00**.

- Add the text shown in Figure 9.12 and resize the graph as necessary.

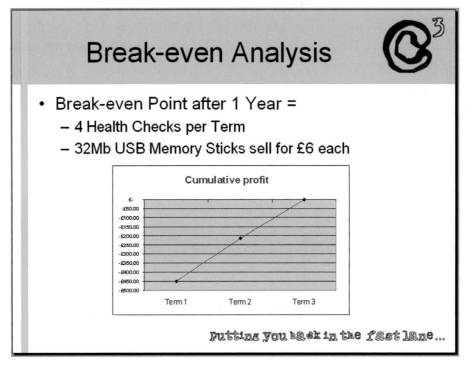

Figure 9.12: Break-even analysis on slide 8

Complete the presentation text by adding the last two slides, 9 and 10, as shown in Figure 9.13.

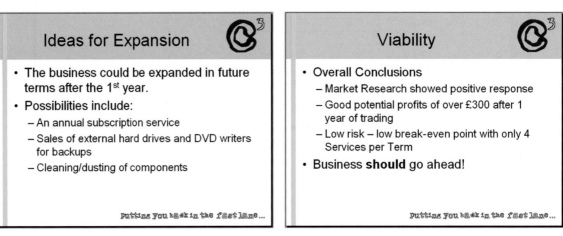

Figure 9.13: Slides 9 and 10

Save the presentation again.

Adding slide transitions

Slide transitions are the way in which one slide changes to the next. There is a variety of different effects you can apply to the slides for different transitions.

For this presentation you need to use a more subtle type of transition so as not to distract the attention of the investment committee away from the actual content of the presentation.

Slide Sorter
View button

▶ Click the **Slide Sorter View** button in the bottom left of the screen or go to **View**, **Slide Sorter**.

▶ Click the **Transition** button on the **Slide Sorter** toolbar.

Figure 9.14: Transition button

▶ Select the **Fade Smoothly** transition and make sure that the **Speed** is set to **Fast**.

Figure 9.15: Adding a Fade Smoothly transition

▶ Click **Apply to All Slides**.

Adding sounds

At this stage you could also add sounds to your presentation. However, it is best not to in this case because it would distract the attention of the investment committee and could make the presentation seem less professional.

 Close the **Slide Transition** window.

Adding animation

Once again, it is best to minimise the effects in order to focus on the content but you could add one subtle animation to the strapline image. If the image on the **Slide Master** is animated, it will reproduce the same effect on all slides.

 Click on **View, Master, Slide Master**.

 Select the **Strapline** image and click **Slide Show, Custom Animation** on the main menu.

 In the **Custom Animation** window, and with the **Strapline** image highlighted, click the **Add Effect** button.

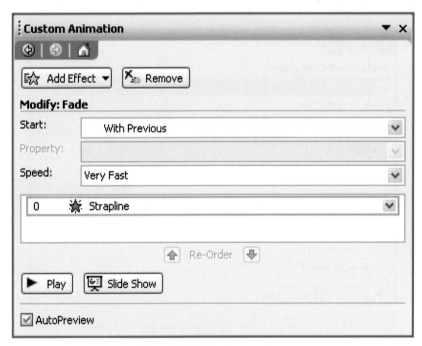

Figure 9.16: Animating an object

 Select **Fade** from **Entrance** effects.

 In the **Start** box select **With Previous** and change the **Speed** to **Very Fast**.

 Close the **Custom Animation** window.

Press **F5** to try out the presentation with the effects added so far.

Press **Esc** to exit the slide show.

Inserting a hyperlink

A presentation of this nature wouldn't often need hyperlinks, but in order to show what they are you can add one to the logo which will take you back to the first slide in the presentation. This could be useful if you ever needed to go back and explain anything after the presentation in response to any questions from the audience.

The **Slide Master** window should already be open. If not go to **View**, **Master**, **Slide Master**.

Select the **C3 Logo** image and click on **Slide Show**, **Action Settings** on the main menu.

In the **Action Settings** window select **Hyperlink to First Slide**.

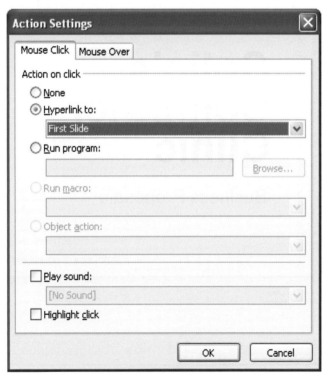

Figure 9.17: Adding Action Settings

Save the presentation and view the show. Test out the hyperlink on the **C3 Logo**.

Select **View**, **Normal** to exit the **Master View**.

Adding speaker notes to a presentation

Speaker notes are notes written about each of the slides. They contain information that you do not want to actually put on the slide but you want to mention as part of your presentation speech. By creating speaker notes you can make sure that you remember everything you wanted to say.

In **Normal** view, you can see a box across the bottom of the screen. This is for adding speaker notes. You can then print out the slides with these underneath, to help you with your speech.

Select the first slide and add the following notes:

Figure 9.18: Adding speaker notes

 Add some more notes for the other slides. The notes for the next two slides could be:

Slide 2:

Mention home visit service by bicycle (5 mile radius).

- *Explain how many people this will roughly cover.*
- *Number of schools in catchment.*

Slide 3:

Recognition from major national newspaper that this is a potential concern of every computer owner.

Trouble-free computing very simple:

- *enable an automatic updating program for your virus checker*
- *get a firewall installed*
- *download free spyware and adware protection software*
- *regular backups.*

External hard disks can be found for less than £40 with 30Gb of storage.

DVD Re-writers available at a similar price.

Printing speaker notes

 Select **File**, **Print**.

 In the **Print** dialogue box, change the **Print what** setting to **Notes Pages**.

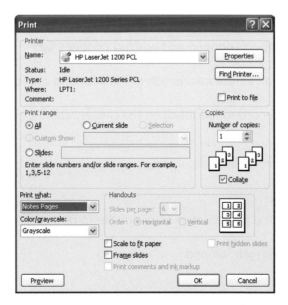

Figure 9.19: Printing notes pages

Printing handouts

It is often a good idea to provide handouts to your audience members so that they can write notes themselves and have something to refer back to after the presentation of each slide.

 To print handouts select **File**, **Print** and in the **Print** dialogue box change the **Print what** setting to **Handouts** (in the same way as you did for **Notes Pages**).

 If you change the **Slides per page** to **3**, it will also give the audience some space next to each slide to make notes.

Figure 9.20: Printing handouts

 Save and close the presentation.

You have now completed the presentation. Now all you have to do is go away and practise your speech!

Good Marks... ✓

You will get good marks if you:

- have selected appropriate evidence for your presentation

- have included everything required and nothing unnecessary

- have demonstrated an astute awareness of the intended audience and purpose

- have received and recorded feedback on the presentation.

Bad Marks... ✗

You will lose marks if you:

- have not converted the presentation to a .pps file to be viewed via the eportfolio

- make it difficult to navigate around.

Chapter 10 – Creating business documents

Types of document

A business will need several types of document, each of which will include the logo and corporate colours to reinforce the corporate identity. Documents will include:

- letterhead
- invoice
- receipt
- compliments slip
- business card
- agenda

Working in a group

For your project you will be working as part of a group. Your group must get together and decide which of the documents are required by the SPB and who will produce each one. It is not necessary for each person to produce all of them, but everyone in the group should produce at least one template.

Ask for feedback from other team members and make any changes that the group decides to be necessary. It is essential that all of the templates produced by the group have a consistent appearance. You will need to include everyone's template in your own eportfolio, so it is vital that that you encourage everyone to do their best! Remember to identify which templates are your own work.

Tip:

Record the outcome of your group's decisions in your project diary.

Producing a template

A template is a part-finished document that contains certain items which stay the same each time you use it. For example, a business letter could be based on a template that already contains the logo, company address and contact details. All you would then need to do is add the text for that particular letter.

Microsoft Word contains some sample templates for you to use if you don't have your own company style.

 Open **Word** and select **File, New**.

 In the **New Document** window, select **Templates on my computer** or **General Templates** if you are using an earlier version of Word.

Have a look at some of the templates available. These are pretty bland since they are for use with any company. You will create a new template that will be unique to your company.

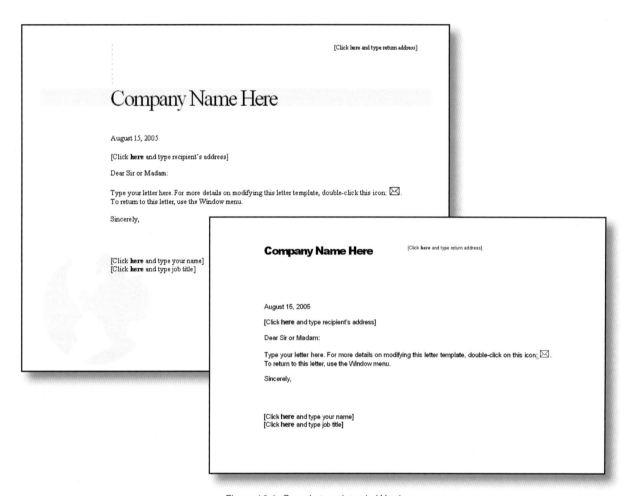

Figure 10.1: Sample templates in Word

The advantages of using templates

The advantages of using templates include:

- all your documents look more professional because they have a consistent appearance
- documents take less time to create because standard items, layout and formatting are already in place.

Creating a letter template in Word

▶ Open **Word** if it is not open already.

It is often a good idea to put all of the components of the template in the header and footer view so that you can't move them around accidentally when you are using the template to write a letter.

▶ Select **View**, **Header and Footer** from the main menu.

▶ Now select **Insert**, **Picture**, **From File**.

▶ Find your **Strapline.gif** file and insert it in the top left of the page inside the margin. Resize it to fit the area.

▶ Do the same with **Logo.gif** file and position it as shown in Figure 10.2.

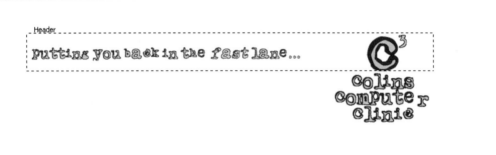

Figure 10.2: Adding template components to the header

▶ Scroll down the page to the **Footer** and add the address and contact details of the company as shown in Figure 10.3.

Figure 10.3: Adding template components to the footer

▶ Format the text as **Arial**, size **8**.

▶ Add a horizontal blue line using the **Line** tool for added effect.

▶ To make the **3** in **C3** smaller and positioned to the top right, highlight the **3** and select **Format**, **Font** from the main menu.

▶ In the **Font** dialogue box, check the **Superscript** box and click **OK**.

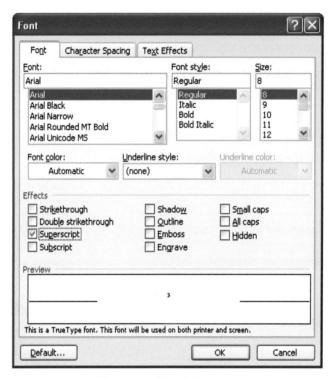

Figure 10.4: Font dialogue box

Adding symbols

For a little more effect you can add symbols indicating the postal, e-mail and web addresses.

- Position the cursor to the left of the **21** in the postal address.
- Click on **Insert**, **Symbol.** The **Symbols** box appears.
- Make sure that **Wingdings** font is selected and choose the **Envelope** symbol, as shown in Figure 10.5.

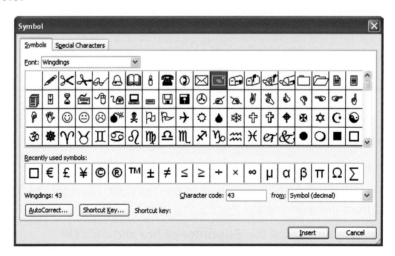

Figure 10.5: Symbols box

- Click **Insert**.

- Repeat the operation to add telephone, computer and e-mail symbols. You can just use a **Bold @** character on the keyboard for the e-mail symbol.

Figure 10.6: The template footer

- **Shade** all the contact details **Dark Blue** and make the company name **Bold**.

Adding placeholders

You can add a few simple placeholders to your letter to ensure that you always position items in your letters in the same place on the page. You will be able to replace these placeholders with the proper details when you use the template.

- Double-click in the centre of the page to get out of the **Header and Footer View**.

- Select **Edit, Select All** from the menu and choose **Arial** font, size **12**.

This will make sure that all text on this template will be the same – your new company font style!

- Add placeholders by typing them in as shown in Figure 10.7 below.

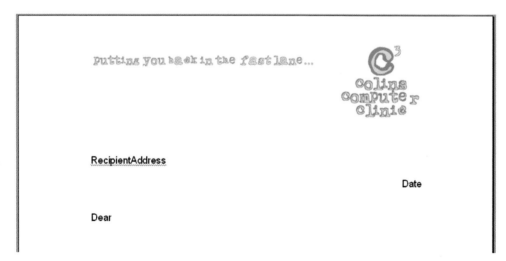

Figure 10.7: Adding placeholders

Saving the document as a template

This is the important bit! You need to tell **Word** that you intend this to be a template for creating future documents rather than just another regular document.

- From the main menu, click **File**, **Save As**.
- Select **Document Template** from the **Save as type** box.
- You will see the default **Templates** folder appear in the **Save in** box.
- Name the file **C3 Letterhead** and click on **Save**.

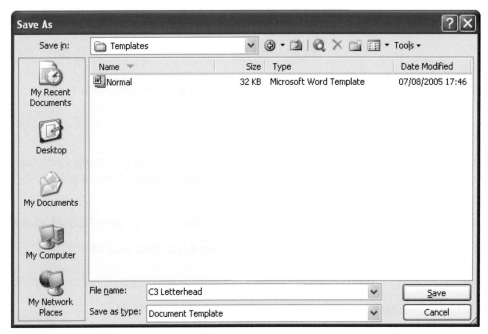

Figure 10.8: Saving a document as a template

 Tip:

It may not be possible to save a template file in the **Templates** folder on the network that you are using. If not, save the file in your own folder as a document, not a template. To use the template, select **New from existing document**.

- **Close** the template file.

Note:

Save the file again on a separate disk as a backup. You can never have too many copies and you would be very annoyed if you lost your only one – especially after reading this note!

Using the new template

- Click on **File**, **New**.
- Click on **Templates on my computer** in the **New Document** window.
- Select the **C3 Letterhead** file and click **OK**.
- Now you can start typing out a letter with all your company details already on it.

Business cards

Business cards are extremely useful even for a sole trader – a business owned and run by just one person. They can be handed out to potential and existing customers, suppliers and other contacts. They provide a handy way of supplying the person's home address, e-mail address and telephone numbers to someone who may want to contact them at a later date.

When you design your business card, you need to think about the image you want to project: how do you want your business to be perceived? Serious, funky, modern, casual, sophisticated, expensive, or cheap and cheerful? Think about its purpose and intended audience.

Think about how the business card will be used – what size should it be? You should look at other people's business cards and analyse them before designing your own.

Creating a business card in Publisher

- Open **Microsoft Publisher** and create a blank document.
- Select **File**, **Page Setup** from the main menu. The **Page Setup** dialogue box appears.

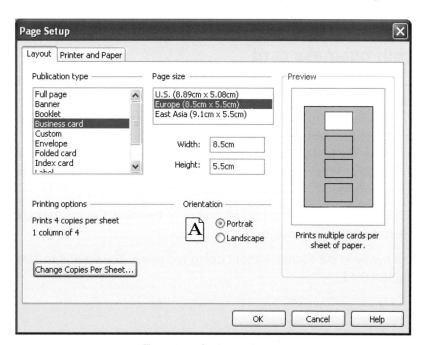

Figure 10.9: Setting up the page

- Select **Business card** and make sure that the **European Page size** is selected.

- Click the **Change Copies per Sheet** button.

- Change the margins to those shown in Figure 10.10 in order to squeeze on an extra 4 cards per sheet.

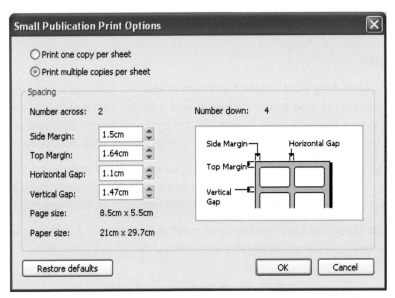

Figure 10.10: Changing the print options

- Click **OK**.

- Use the **Zoom** tool to go to about **200%**.

Designing your business card

Now you can start designing your business card. Don't expect to get it perfect first time. You will need to rough it out on paper first and then transfer those ideas onto the computer. After this you should save it as a first draft, then print out a copy and highlight areas for improvement. This could involve moving images around, creating more or fewer areas of colour, or simply correcting spelling. Once you have made these corrections on the computer you should save it again under a different file name. This will show your sequence of development and refinement of the business card, for top marks.

- Start by adding the full logo to the top left corner of the card. Go to **Insert**, **Picture**, **From File** and select the **Logo.gif** image.

- Resize it to fit neatly in the corner without being too small. You want it to stand out – as shown in Figure 10.11.

Figure 10.11: Inserting and resizing the logo

▶ Now add a little more colour to the card by putting a **Light Green** rectangle down the right-hand side, using the same colour as the **3** in the logo. It is a good idea to stick to the original colour scheme to maintain a consistent brand image.

▶ Now add the **C3 Logo.gif** image and place this in the bottom right corner. Make it hang off the page so that only part of it will print out.

Figure 10.12: Inserting the C3 logo

The C3 logo has added a little too much colour to the business card and needs to be toned down a little. If it is left like this, it may draw the attention of the reader away from the important contact details that you will need to add.

▶ Right-click on the **C3 Logo** and select **Show Picture Toolbar** if it is not already visible.

▶ Click the **Color** button on the **Picture** toolbar and select **Washout**.

▶ Now add the contact details in the bottom left, as shown in Figure 10.13. Make them **Dark Blue**, **Arial**, size **7**.

Color button

Add Colin's name and position, as shown in Figure 10.13 below. Use the same style, with size **11** font.

Figure 10.13: The finished business card.

Try printing the document out to see how the eight business cards fit onto the page.

Save the document as **Business Card.pub**.

Invoices

When a company sells goods or services to an individual or to another business, an invoice is sent. The invoice tells the customer how much to pay and where to send their payment.

You may need to include:

- the company name, address and VAT registration number (if the company has a turnover of, currently, more than £58,000 per year)
- the date
- the invoice number
- the customer's order number (if applicable)
- the customer's account number, name and address
- details of the goods or services being invoiced for
- net amount
- VAT @ 17.5% (if applicable)
- postage and packaging costs (if applicable)
- total amount
- terms of payment and any discount offered.

Figure 10.14 below shows a possible layout for the C3 invoice.

Putting you back in the fast lane...

Colin's Computer Clinic
21 Bishop Road
Friston
BN21 3TU

SALES INVOICE

Mrs S Rawson
83 High Road
Leeds
LS19 5SL

Invoice Date: 05 Sept 2005
Invoice No. 0084
Account No. RAWS001
Order No. 0108

Item No.	Qty	Description	Cost per Item	Total Cost
SERV01	1	First PC Service	£10.00	£10.00
MEM256	2	Memory Stick 256Mb	£16.00	£32.00

Total due £42.00

Terms: Payment is due within 30 days of invoice date.

Figure 10.14: Sample invoice

- Try recreating this invoice, using tabs to line up all of the information correctly.
- Make sure you use a font, font size and colour scheme that is consistent with your house style.

Exercise 1: Designing a logo

Design a new logo for Colin's Computer Clinic.

Look at a collection of business cards and then design a different one for Colin's Computer Clinic, using your own colour scheme, font and logo.

Exercise 2: Presenting a logo

In a group of three or four, present your logo and business card samples to the other members of the group for review. Explain your intended goals, design decisions and purpose. The reviewers should then discuss how well the intended goals and purpose were met. What changes are recommended?

If your group had to adopt one of the logos and business cards, which would you choose? Would you take some ideas from more than one of the samples you are reviewing or showing?

Good Marks... ✓

You will get good marks for your documents if you:

- decide in a group what your templates will look like and who will produce each one

- show an astute awareness of the audience and purpose of each template and make sure the purpose is fulfilled

- have your template reviewed by the group and note down in your project diary what comments were made and how you changed your design in response to feedback

- make sure that your group has produced the complete set of required templates – if one group member has let you down, you will have to reallocate their tasks!

Bad Marks... ✗

You will lose marks if:

- you do not work as a team to develop the template designs

- your group's templates are inconsistent

- the templates do not reinforce the corporate identity.

Once you have collected all your completed market research questionnaires and analysed the results, you will have a better idea of whether your business is likely to succeed. Since you have collected names and addresses, you can also use the data from the completed questionnaires to do some marketing. In this chapter we will look at how you can write a mail merge letter using the spreadsheet data.

Suppose you have bought a large quantity of flash memory sticks and screen wipes, and would like to increase your sales as well as persuade potential customers to book a computer service. One way to do this is to send a personalised letter to everyone who has returned your questionnaire.

Preparing the data source

You can use a database or a spreadsheet as a data source for a mail merge, or you can type the names and addresses into **Word**. For this example you should have a spreadsheet called **PotentialCustomers.xls** created in Chapter 5. This contains the names and addresses of people who returned your questionnaire. You can download the spreadsheet below from the Payne-Gallway website at **www.payne-gallway.co.uk** by clicking on the relevant link in the DiDA section.

	A	B	C	D	E	F	G	H	I	J	K	L
1	Title	FirstName	Surname	Address1	Address2	Town	Postcode	email	PCs	FlashDrive	Slower	Service
2	Mrs	Constance	Corbett	17 Long Street		London	SW4 7RF	c.corbett@talk21.com	1	Yes	Yes	Yes
3	Mrs	William	Melsa	27 Pearcroft Drive		London	SW4 2TH	willmelsa@ntlworld.com	2	No	Yes	Yes
4	Mrs	Sharon	Maxfield	145 Helsden Rd		London	SW3 7YP	bigsharon@yahoo.co.uk	1	No	No	No
5	Mrs	Deidre	Griffin	6 St John's Close		London	SW4 6CV	thegriffins@ntlworld.com	1	No	Yes	Yes
6	Mr	George	Langley	17 Redwing Ave		London	SW3 2KB	georgeLangley231@hot.ail.com	1	No	No	No
7	Miss	Wanda	Patten	21 Long St		London	SW4 7RF	wanda222@hotmail.co.uk	3	No	Yes	Yes
8	Mr	Ken	Souter	Flat 2a	26 Kingsnorth Rd	London	SW5 8GG	kensouter@lineone.net	1	No	Yes	Yes
9	Mr	Brian	Vickers	7 Yalta Rd		London	SW3 7DC	brianFreda@tiscali.com	2	Yes	Yes	No
10	Mrs	Jean	Mendes	5 Fletcher House	Maybush Ave	London	SW4 5SD	jcmendes@hotmail.co.uk	1	Yes	Yes	Yes

Figure 11.1: Spreadsheet of potential customers

Writing the letter

The first step is to compose your letter. You must decide exactly what information you want to impart and how you expect the customers to reply. Will they telephone you, e-mail you or write?

Your letter must look professional and include your logo, company name and contact details. If you have created a template for business letters, you should use it for your **mailshot**.

 Load **Word** and open a new document, using your previously created template if you have one. Alternatively, you could print your letters on pre-printed stationery. We will assume that you are going to use pre-printed stationery in this exercise, so you will start with a blank sheet.

Leave a few blank lines at the top of the page to allow room for the company name and address on the pre-printed stationery and compose a marketing letter to your potential customers. Use Figure 11.2 as a guide.

21st January 2006

Dear

Introductory offer on computer service!

I am pleased to be able to offer you an introductory service to keep your PC running smoothly, for just **£9.00** for all services booked before February 28th. The service will include virus checking and removal, blocking pop-up advertisements and removing unwanted spyware.

Please telephone me on 01323 746635 (after 5pm or on weekends), or email colin@paynegallway.co.uk/c3 to arrange a convenient time for me to call round to your home.

I can also offer some fantastic prices on flash memory sticks and optical mice:

128Mb Flash drives £10.00
256Mb Flash drives £15.00
Optical Mouse   £20.00

To place an order, simply phone or email me and I will deliver to your door at a convenient time.

Yours sincerely

Colin Blake

Figure 11.2: Example marketing letter

Performing the mail merge

 From the **Tools** menu select **Letters and Mailings**, **Mail Merge Wizard**.

There are six steps involved in setting up a mail merge:

Step 1:   Select the type of document you are working on.

Step 2:   Set up and display your document.

Step 3:   Select recipients – open or create the list of names and addresses to whom the document is being sent.

Step 4:   Write your letter (if you have not already done so) and add recipient information to the letter.

Step 5:   Preview the letters.

Step 6:   Complete the merge.

Step 1: Select the type of document

On the right-hand side of the screen, the **Mail Merge** panel will appear.

Figure 11.3: The Mail Merge panel

Leave **Letters** selected.

At the bottom of the panel, click **Next: Starting document**.

Step 2: Set up and display your document

Figure 11.4: Setting up your document

Leave **Use the current document** selected.

At the bottom of the panel, click **Next: Select recipients**.

Step 3: Select recipients

Figure 11.5: Selecting recipients

Leave **Use an existing list** selected.

Click the **Browse** icon. Navigate to your **Excel** spreadsheet, **PotentialCustomers.xls**. From the **Select Table** dialogue box select the sheet containing the source data and click **OK**.

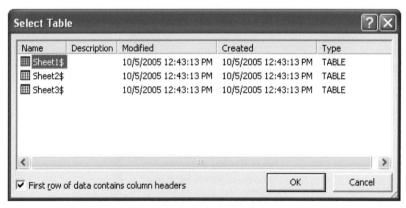

Figure 11.6: Select Table dialogue box

Click **OK**.

In the next window – the **Mail Merge Recipients** dialogue box – you can select who is to receive the letter. You might choose to miss out people who said they are not interested in a computer service, for example, or you may decide to mail everyone in the hope that they will change their mind.

In this example we will send the letter to everyone who returned the questionnaire.

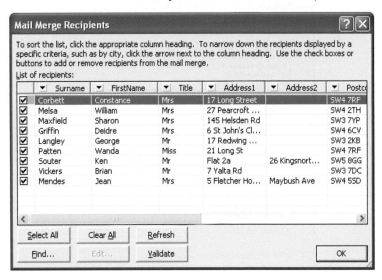

Figure 11.7: Mail Merge Recipients dialogue box

- Click **Select All** and then click **OK**.

- Click **Next: Write your letter** at the bottom of the **Mail Merge** panel.

Step 4: Write your letter

The body of your letter is already written. You now need to add the mail merge fields to personalise each letter.

Figure 11.8: Adding mail merge fields

- Click in your letter, two lines above the date.

- Click the icon for **Address block**; the **Insert Address Block** dialogue box appears.

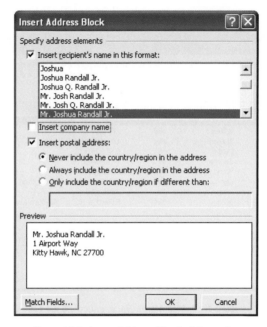

Figure 11.9: Insert Address Block dialogue box

You will be given various options for how you want the address to appear. You don't need the company name or the country.

⊙ Select the options as shown in Figure 11.9 above and click **OK**.

⊙ Now select the word **Dear** in the letter. This will be replaced by a standard greeting line.

⊙ Click **Greeting Line**; the **Greeting Line** dialogue box appears.

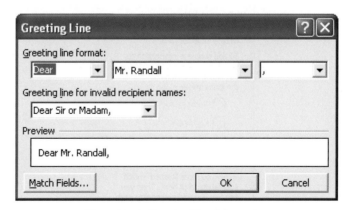

Figure 11.10: Greeting Line dialogue box

⊙ Leave the default options and click **OK**.

The first few lines of your letter will look like this:

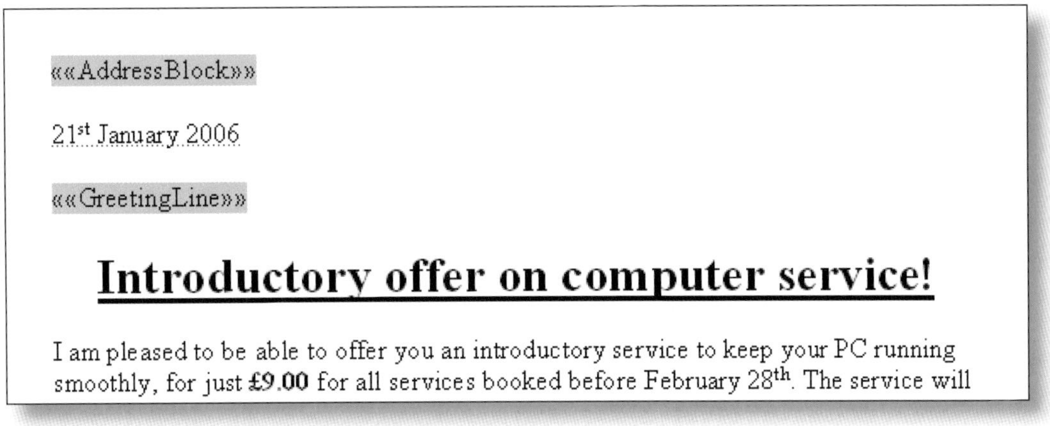

««AddressBlock»»

21st January 2006

««GreetingLine»»

Introductory offer on computer service!

I am pleased to be able to offer you an introductory service to keep your PC running smoothly, for just £9.00 for all services booked before February 28th. The service will

Figure 11.11: Example letter

 Click **Next: Preview your letters** at the bottom of the **Mail Merge** panel.

Step 5: Preview your letters

The first letter will appear, as shown in Figure 11.12.

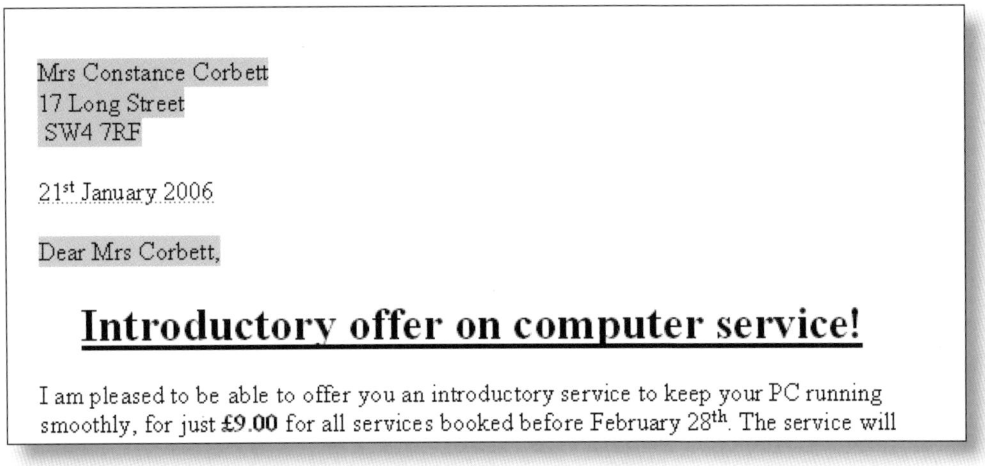

Mrs Constance Corbett
17 Long Street
SW4 7RF

21st January 2006

Dear Mrs Corbett,

Introductory offer on computer service!

I am pleased to be able to offer you an introductory service to keep your PC running smoothly, for just £9.00 for all services booked before February 28th. The service will

Figure 11.12: Previewing your letter

You will notice that the **Town** field is missing. You can correct this in one of two ways:

Method 1

Go back to Step 4 and replace the address block. This time, click the **Match Fields** button shown in Figure 11.9. In the **Match Fields** dialogue box you will be able to match your field names with the standard field names.

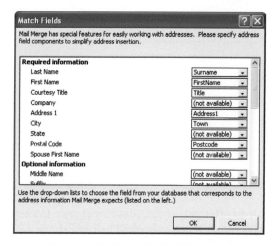

Figure 11.13: Match Fields dialogue box

You can also try the next method but it is fiddly and does not always give entirely satisfactory results.

Method 2

In Step 4, insert the fields one by one. We will do this.

Return to Step 4 by pressing the **Previous: Write your letter** link at the bottom of the **Mail Merge** panel.

Delete the **Address Block** field in your letter. Leave the cursor on that line.

Click the **More Items** icon; the **Insert Merge Field** dialogue box appears.

Figure 11.14: Insert Merge Field dialogue box

With the **Title** field selected, click **Insert**.

Select the **FirstName** field and click **Insert**.

▶ Select in turn the **Surname**, **Address1**, **Address2**, **Town** and **Postcode** fields and insert each of them.

Your address block will now look like this:

«Title»«FirstName»«Surname»«Address1»«Address2»«Town»«Postcode»

Figure 11.15: Address block

You need to insert spaces and new lines so that it looks like this:

«Title» «FirstName» «Surname»
«Address1»
«Address2»
«Town»
«Postcode»

Figure 11.16: Address block with spaces and lines added

▶ Now go to the next step and preview your letters again. You can look at each letter in turn to make sure that they all look correct.

Mr Ken Souter
Flat 2a
26 Kingsnorth Rd
London
SW5 8GG

21st January 2006

Dear Mr Souter,

Introductory offer on computer service!

I am pleased to be able to offer you an introductory service to keep your PC running smoothly, for just £9.00 for all services booked before February 28th. The service will

Figure 11.17: Mail merge preview screen

▶ Click **Next: Complete the merge** when you are satisfied all is correct.

▶ **Save** your mail merge letter. There is no need to print any letters.

In this chapter you will look at using some of the features of e-mail software and ways of finding information on the Internet more efficiently.

E-mail software

Microsoft Outlook is a standard piece of communications software that comes as part of the **Windows** package. **Outlook** works by organising all of your e-mails belonging to another account such as **Hotmail**, **Gmail** or **AOL**. These are all examples of web-based e-mail providers with a wealth of features that can make organising your business communication much easier.

Setting up an e-mail account

If you don't already have an e-mail account set up for you, try visiting one of the web-based e-mail providers listed above and signing up for a new, free account. You will need to submit your personal details such as name and location and you will be asked to choose a user name or email address for yourself. The whole registration process can take up to 30 minutes to complete. For **Hotmail**, go to **www.hotmail.co.uk**.

Once you have set up an account you can begin using it to send and receive e-mails from other people.

Receiving and reading new e-mail messages

Once you have set up a new account you will often automatically receive an e-mail welcoming you to the service. After this you will need to give your new e-mail address to friends and your business contacts.

 Go to your **Inbox** to check any mail you have received.|

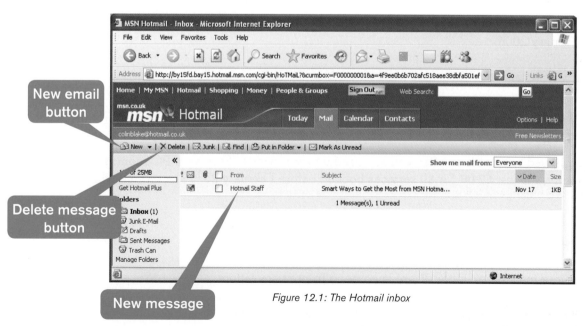

Figure 12.1: The Hotmail inbox

In most e-mail services, new mail will be displayed in bold. To read the mail, click on the name of the message sender. In Figure 12.1, this is **Hotmail Staff**. The message should then be displayed.

After you have read the message, you can either delete it or return to the **Inbox**.

Sending a message

To send a message click on the **New** button or the **Compose** button, depending on which e-mail provider you are using.

▶ Click on the **New** button to compose a new message.

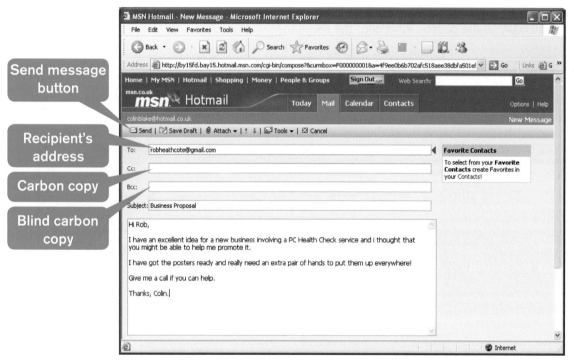

Send message button

Recipient's address

Carbon copy

Blind carbon copy

Figure 12.2: Creating a new message

Type the recipient's address in the **To** box at the top of the message and the message subject in the **Subject** box.

Enter your message in the main area of the screen.

When you have finished, click on the **Send** button to send the message.

> **Note:**
>
> **Cc** stands for **Carbon Copy**. The **Cc** box allows you to send the same message to another person at the same time. You can add as many other e-mail addresses in here as you like, separated by a semi-colon (;). **Bcc** stands for **Blind Carbon Copy**. The **Bcc** box allows you to send the same message to another person at the same time, but the other recipients will not know that the message was sent to the recipient in the **Bcc** box.

Attaching a file to a message

To attach a file, click the **Attach** button. This is often accompanied by a paperclip symbol.

Follow the instructions given and select the file you wish to attach.

The filename of the attachment should be displayed above the message text and a paperclip symbol will often appear next to the message as well.

Replying to a message

You can reply to a message very simply by clicking the **Reply** button on the message. If the message was originally sent to you as part of a group, you can click a **Reply to All** button. This will send the reply to everyone who received the same message as you. The **Reply** button will only send the reply to the person who sent the message.

Setting up an address book

In **Hotmail** there is a **Contacts** button which you can click on to view a current list of contacts and then edit them or add new contacts.

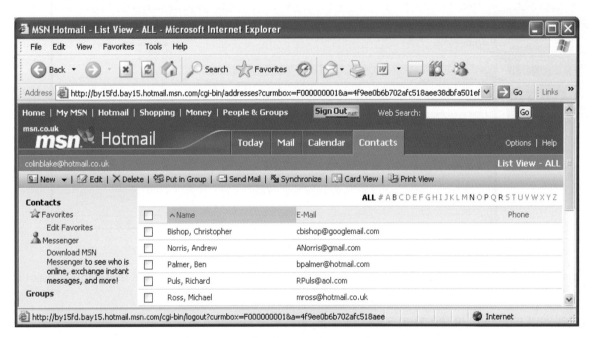

Figure 12.3: A list of contacts in an e-mail account

Having a list of contacts available makes it easier to send messages to these people. When composing a new message, it is now possible to click on the contact's name to add his or her address rather than having to remember the person's details and type them in manually.

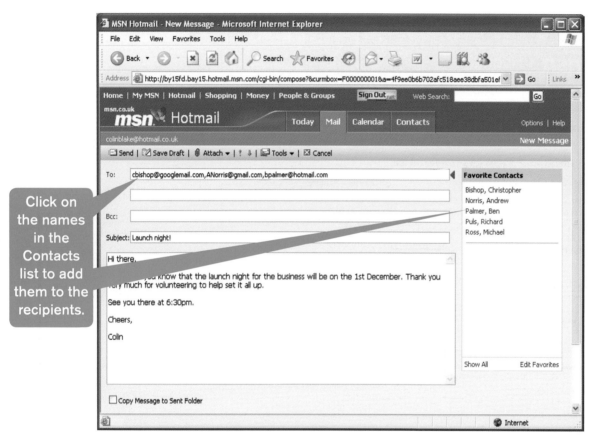

Figure 12.4: Using a list of contacts to enter e-mail addresses

Grouping contacts

If you have a particular group of contacts that you regularly e-mail, it is a good idea to add them to a specific group. This way any messages meant for those in the group can be sent by selecting the group name, rather than each individual e-mail address.

In the **Contacts** page, there is usually an option to define a **New Group** and add contacts from your list of addresses.

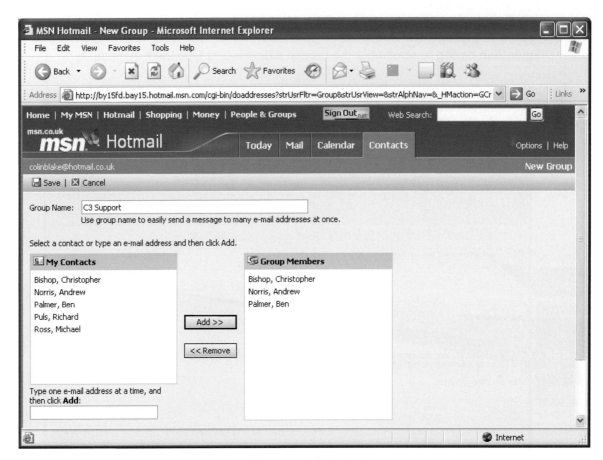

Figure 12.5: Defining e-mail distribution lists or groups

Setting the importance of an e-mail

If you are sending an e-mail, you can set the message to appear as urgent or important when it arrives in the recipient's inbox.

Simply click the **Importance** button before you send the message. The e-mail should arrive in the recipient's inbox with an exclamation mark beside it marking it as urgent.

The Importance button

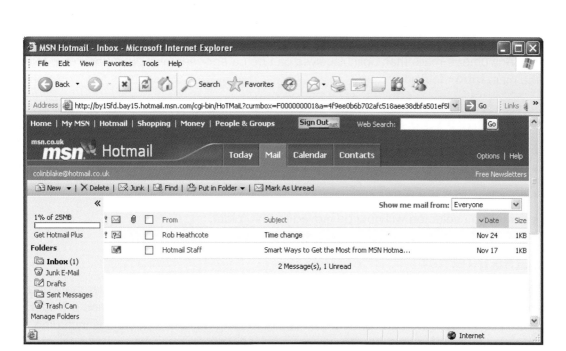

Figure 12.6: Receiving an important message

Setting up folders to organise your e-mails

You can set up folders in your e-mail package in a similar way to the folders in **Windows Explorer**. These can be used to store e-mails in categories that will make them easier to find at a later date.

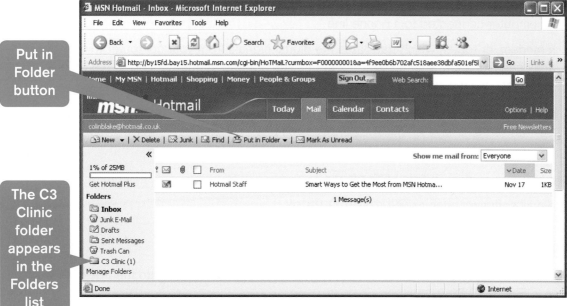

Figure 12.7: Setting up a C3 Clinic folder to store related e-mails

In Figure 12.7, a new folder called **C3 Clinic** has been added to store all e-mails that relate to the company. Any other e-mails that Colin receives can be categorised and put in their own folders or left in the main **Inbox** folder.

Adding e-mails to a new folder

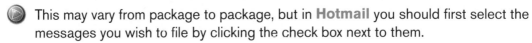 This may vary from package to package, but in **Hotmail** you should first select the messages you wish to file by clicking the check box next to them.

Next click on **Put in Folder** and select **C3 Clinic**.

The messages you selected will now be moved to that folder.

Using the Internet

The Internet consists of a huge number of computers connected together all over the world. You can connect to the Internet only at certain points, via a phone or cable service provider. If you have a wireless adaptor you can connect from an increasing number of locations including, for example, train stations and libraries.

The best known thing about the Internet is the **World Wide Web**. This consists of hundreds of millions of web pages stored on computers all over the world, which you can access from your own computer. Virtually all large companies and organisations have websites, as do many small companies and private individuals.

Hardware and software for Internet access

To access the Internet you will need some hardware:

- a computer connected to a phone line

- a modem, or router, which translates the digital signals from your computer to an analogue signal transmitted over the phone line; another modem/router at the other end translates the signal back from analogue to digital

- alternatively, you may use an ISDN or broadband line; you can also connect to the Internet using a WAP phone or TV and set-top box.

You will need some software:

- a browser, such as **Internet Explorer**

- e-mail software, such as **Microsoft Outlook**.

Using a web address

If you know the website address, the easiest way to get there is to type it into the **address box**, as shown in Figure 12.8.

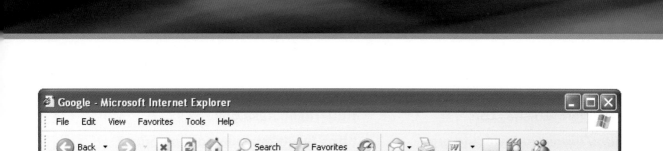

Figure 12.8: Typing a web address

Every web page has a unique address, known as the **URL**, or **Uniform Resource Locator**. This has distinct parts separated by dots, each part having a special significance. A typical address is http://www.bbc.co.uk.

The first part is the protocol used by the Internet for sending and receiving data between computers. The most common protocol is **http://**, which stands for **Hypertext Transfer Protocol**. There's no need to type in **http://** because the browser adds it automatically. Some addresses may have **https://** for a secure page with sensitive information, or **ftp://** for file transfer.

www stands for **World Wide Web** and is in most but not all web page addresses.

bbc.co.uk is the domain name showing the organisation owning the site and has several parts:

- **bbc** is the company name

- **co** is the type of site, in this case a commercial organisation; international company domain names generally end in **.com**; some other codes are **gov** for government, **org** for non-profit organisations, **ac** for educational sites (**edu** in the USA) or **sch** for schools

- If the site is neither **.com** nor US-based, there is usually a country code: **uk** for the UK, **fr** for France, **de** for Germany, **es** for Spain, **ch** for Switzerland, **ie** for Ireland, and so on.

Tip:

New codes that you may see are **biz**, **plc**, **info**, **tv** and **me**.

You will have heard of **dotcom** companies; this is often misspelt as **dot.com**, which would have to be pronounced **dot dot com**.

There may also be the name of a file on the end of the address, such as **/index.htm**. Web pages are written in a language called **HTML** (for **Hypertext Markup Language**) and each page is a file, usually ending in **.htm**.

Tip:

To go to an address in the format **www.*name*.com**, just type *name*, hold down **Ctrl** and press **Enter**. The rest is put in for you!

111

Below are some sample URLs – you can probably guess what they belong to.

http://www.disney.com   ftp://ftp.hq.nasa.gov

http://www.worldwildlife.org   http://www.museum-london.org.uk

http://www.cam.ac.uk   http://www.harvard.edu

http://www.payne-gallway.co.uk   http://www.louvre.fr

Hyperlinks

Most web pages on the Internet have hyperlinks on them, which enable you to jump to another page or even back to the top of the same page if it is quite long. When you move the mouse over a hyperlink, the pointer changes from an arrow to a hand in order to indicate that it is over a 'hot' area. These are usually underlined blue text but could also be pictures. When you click on one of these links, the browser jumps to that page.

 Try logging on to **www.google.co.uk** and moving your mouse pointer over the page. There are several hyperlinks underlined here, as shown in Figure 12.9.

Figure 12.9: Google home page

Using a search engine

Google is a good example of a search engine. A search engine is software that allows you to type a word or phrase into a box then search the Internet and view all the results that it finds.

Some sites have a built-in search engine of their own to search for things within that site.

Search engines keep an index of keywords. Special programs – known as **crawlers**, **spiders** or **bots** – continually run all over the Web collecting keywords from each website. These embedded keywords (called **meta tags**) are invisible in normal view but are put on the site by the designer, so as to be found by crawlers and cause the site to pop up on search results pages as often as possible. With vague or misleading keywords a page will often appear unexpectedly.

 Enter the address **www.google.co.uk**.

 Try a search – enter **virus security** into the **Search** box.

At the time of writing, Google finds over 92 million references. Now that is information overload! However, the first few results direct you to some key sites.

Figure 12.10: Using Google

Refining a search

With such a large number of results you will need to refine your search. You need to cut down the number of results that are not relevant.

▶ Try typing **virus security –medical**. Be careful not to put a space after the minus (–) sign.

This finds all the sites that include the words **virus** and **security** but do NOT include the word **medical**.

This reduces the number of results by about 15 million, but still gives 77 million links!

An alternative is to use the **Google Advanced Search**.

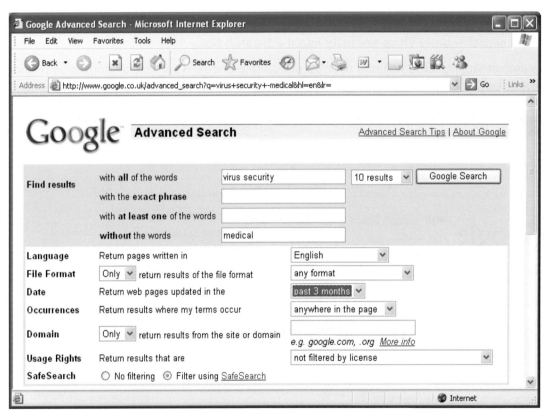

Figure 12.11: Refining your search with Google's Advanced Search feature

Tips for searching

You must take some care in setting up your search query – you need to communicate exactly what you want to find. Remember these useful tips:

- If possible do not use connecting words like **the** and **and**.

- Check your spelling.

- Be specific. Try a few different word combinations.

- Using quotation marks around a phrase will get more accurate results.

- Several search engines (e.g. **www.ask.com**) allow you to ask a direct question and then search for the results.

- Try using Boolean operators such as **AND**, **OR**, **NOT**, or the + and − signs to refine your search.

- Remember that after an initial search you may have to make a further search within those results.

Saving your results

You will often need to save or print the results of your research to refer to later. You can usually select the text on a web page, right-click on it and select **Copy**, then paste the text into your own word-processed document.

> **Note:**
>
> Make a note of the website address you copied any text from so that you can acknowledge the source of your information.

Saving a web page

Internet Explorer will allow you to save any web page to the hard drive of your computer or to a floppy disk. The saved page is just like any other document so you can open the browser and view the page while you are working offline.

▶ Open the page in **Internet Explorer** and choose **Save As** from the **File** menu.

▶ The **Save Web Page** dialogue box appears, as shown below.

Figure 12.12: Saving a web page

⊚ Navigate to the folder in which you want to store your saved documents. Enter a **File name**.

⊚ Make sure that **Web Page, complete** appears in the **Save as type** box. Click **Save**. You have saved the whole web page, including any pictures.

To view the saved web page:

⊚ Open **Internet Explorer**.

⊚ From the **File** menu, select **Work Offline**. From the same menu, select **Open**.

Tip:

If you are working offline, **Internet Explorer** will not try to connect to the Internet. You should change this setting back when you have finished browsing your files.

⊚ Click the **Browse** button to navigate to the folder where you saved the web page and related graphics. Select the file with the **Internet Explorer** symbol and click **Open**.

⊚ Click **OK** on the **Open** dialogue box.

Sometimes you may just want to save a picture from a website.

⊚ Right-click the image and choose **Save Picture As**.

⊚ After selecting file type, find the folder in which you want to save the picture and click **Save**.

Storing the URL

Sometimes you may want to store the URL (address) of a particular web page so that you can return to it quickly at any time. In **Netscape** or **Firefox**, this is called saving a **bookmark**. In **Internet Explorer** you add the page to a list of **Favorites**.

You can practise adding a page to the **Favorites** list and then using the saved link.

⊚ Load **Internet Explorer**.

⊚ Click the **Favorites** button on the toolbar. (If you haven't got one, you can press **Ctrl+I** instead.)

Figure 12.13: The Favorites button in Internet Explorer

The **Favorites** pane will open on the left-hand side of the screen; this is shown in Figure 12.14.

Now suppose you have found a page that you want to save.

- Click the **Add** button (see Figure 12.14) or select **Favorites**, **Add to Favorites** from the menu.

- An **Add Favorite** dialogue box will appear, showing you the name that will appear in your **Favorites** list. You can edit this if you wish.

Figure 12.14: Adding a Favorite site

Tip:

It is a very good idea to store any sites that you have used information or images from as **Favorites**, or save them to your hard disk to view later. This way you have an easy reference to your sources when you come to acknowledge them in the eportfolio.

Chapter 13 – Advertising your product

Marketing is a major expense for most businesses but one that is essential to promote their products or increase people's awareness of them.

Marketing can encompass everything from e-mailing customers, going to trade fairs, producing TV commercials, to creating a good public image by donating to charity or sponsoring events. Advertising is one form of marketing.

Different methods of advertising

There are several ways that you can advertise your products. These include using direct advertising such as displaying posters and TV commercials, or using more subtle methods such as painting your logo on shopping bags or delivery vans.

Methods of advertising you could use include:

- leaflets
- flyers
- posters
- movies/promotional trailers
- presentation information points
- packaging
- websites
- banners
- shopping bags
- car stickers.

You could use some or all of these methods in your advertising campaign. Each of these methods will hit a slightly different segment of your market and therefore need to be carefully designed with those people in mind.

Exercise: Identifying a market

Try to identify the potential target market for each of the methods of advertising listed above for **Colin's Computer Clinic**.

What are the advantages and disadvantages to a company of using each of these methods? Consider the effectiveness of each method and not just their initial cost.

Creating successful advertising

For your advertisement to be successful you must create something that first attracts the attention of the potential customers and then persuades them to read the information available.

There are several things you should include or consider in order to achieve this:

- your corporate identity
- structure
- balance
- colour
- composition
- message
- emotion
- promotional words such as Special Offer, Free and BOGOF (Buy One Get One Free).

You should also make sure that your contact details are clearly displayed.

Exercise: Researching advertisements

In groups look at Figures 13.1–13.3 and discuss whether each of them has been successful at attracting your attention and making you want to know more.

Figure 13.1: Tower Bridge Exhibition magazine advertising

Figure 13.2: Visit London magazine advertising

Figure 13.3: British Heart Foundation

Target audience

In your groups you must each decide which particular audience to target with your advertising. Each member of the group should produce their own advertising pack of at least two different items from the list earlier in the chapter (on page 118) and include this pack in their eportfolio.

The target audience for the poster and flyer shown in Figure 13.4 will be the parents of school pupils when they arrive at a parent's evening.

Below is an example of a poster for the company. You should always save the first draft as a separate file before you make any modifications following feedback.

Figure 13.4: The C3 Poster (first and second draft)

Exercise: Designing a poster

Design another poster using the logo and colour scheme that you developed earlier.

In your group, review all the designs produced by your team and select a poster and flyer to create in **Publisher**. You could put this in your eportfolio.

In order to advertise your products or services really effectively you will need a website. This will enable potential customers to find out more about your company and to contact you. They may look up your company on the Internet after seeing your advertising.

Researching web design

It is important to look at the way that other websites are designed before leaping into designing your own. You may see some great features that you could use in yours and discover some effective ways to organise each page.

Exercise: Deciding what works

Look for good and bad examples of web design on the Internet. Ask yourself the following questions:

- Are some websites easier to navigate than others? If so, why?
- What features do you like?

Here is a web page from the Payne-Gallway website **www.payne-gallway.co.uk**.

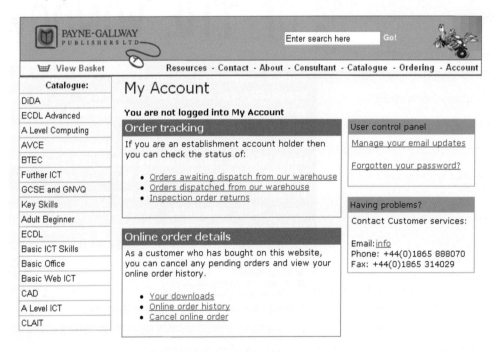

Figure 14.1: Part of the Payne-Gallway website

This web page contains some typical design features that many sites adopt. For example, it has a bar across the top with the company name, colour scheme and logo. It also has a navigation bar down the left-hand side with links to other pages within the site.

Good tips for web design include:

- Keep it simple
- Try to limit the file size and quantity of images, to help download speeds
- Avoid making the site too wide – nobody likes to scroll sideways
- Use the same fonts and styles throughout.

Establishing the components of the C3 website

Each website has a home page and links to other pages. You need to decide what information to put on the home page, what other pages you need and what will go on each one.

For this project, your group needs to produce four web pages. You must discuss what these pages will be and then share the workload by allocating different tasks to each team member. You could ask each member to produce a design and then select the best one.

Tip:

Remember to make a note of your group's decisions in your project diary.

The information that will be needed in Colin's website includes:

- company home page
- product details (giving information and prices of computer accessories)
- service details (offering details of the maintenance service)
- contact details (allowing customers to register themselves and find address and telephone details).

Each of these will become a page in the website.

Designing a storyboard

Once you have worked out the different pages that you want on the site, you can start designing the layout and content of each page and decide how the pages will link together.

You can also use the storyboard to draw a preliminary thumbnail sketch of how each page will look, then draw connecting lines to show how they link to each other.

You should use the logo and company colour scheme that you have already come up with. If possible, use colour in your sketches to help visualise the final web pages.

You can download a copy of the following storyboard from **www.payne-gallway.co.uk** (click on the relevant link in the DiDA section) or alternatively create your own in **Word**.

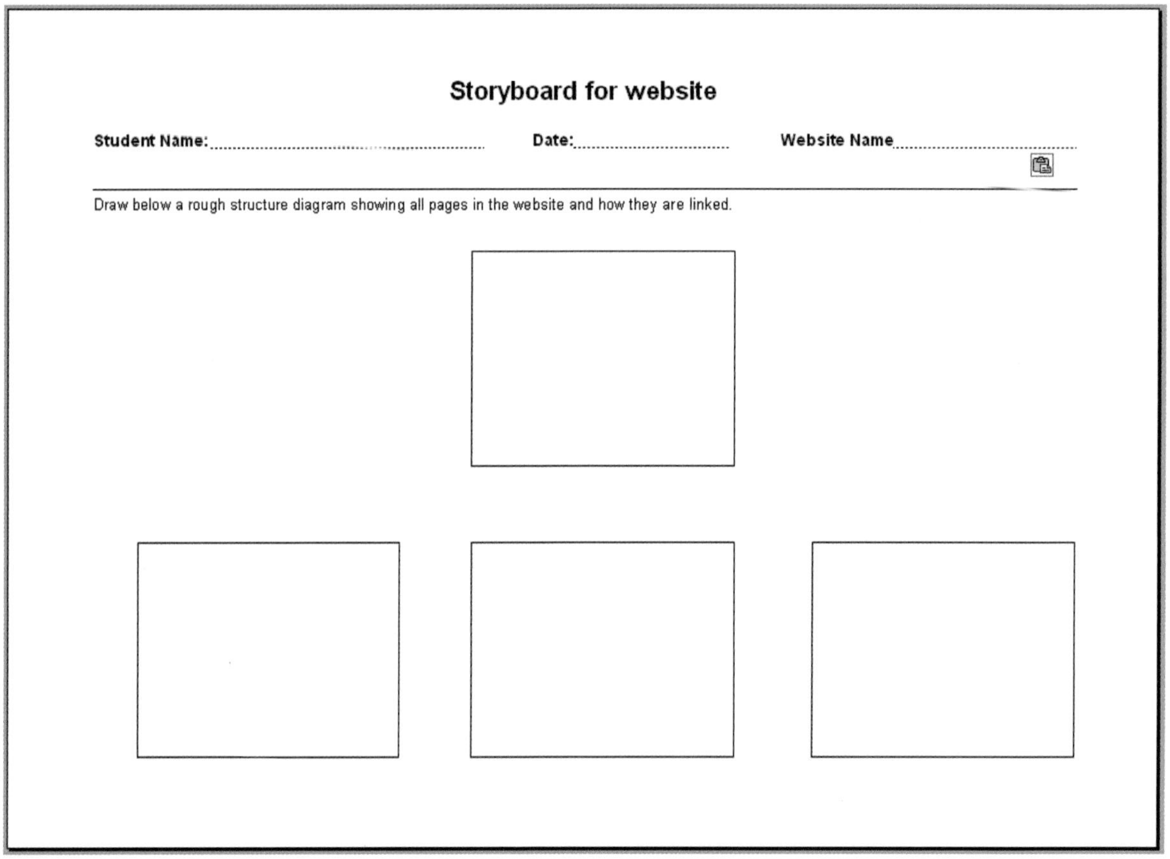

Figure 14.2: Structure chart sheet

Exercise: Planning your website

Download a blank sheet and sketch out some of your design ideas for your website.

Annotate the designs to show possible fonts, styles and colours that are not obvious from your sketches.

If you are working in a group, add notes to specify who is to perform each sub-task.

The plans need to have enough detail for someone else to immediately envisage what the site will be like and be able to constructively criticise it. This useful criticism will then be used to improve the designs further.

An example of a detailed storyboard for a website is shown in Figure 14.3.

Student Name: COLIN BLAKE

Date: 15 MARCH '06

Website Name COMPUTER CLINIC

Draw below a rough structure diagram showing all pages in the website and how they are linked.

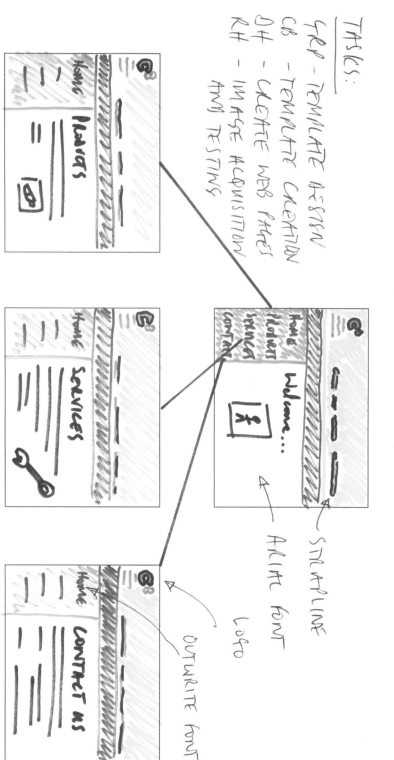

TASKS:

TDP - TEMPLATE DESIGN
CB - TEMPLATE CREATION
DH - CREATE WEB PAGES
RH - IMAGE ACQUISITION AND TESTING

Figure 14.3: Detailed storyboard sheet

125

Good Marks... ✓

You will get good marks if you:

- produce a storyboard for your website
- make sure the design is: complete, including content and navigation; suitable for potential customers in style and language
- show your individual contribution to this task
- monitor your progress and make sure you meet your deadlines
- keep a project diary of your day-to-day tasks.

Bad Marks... ✗

You will lose marks if:

- your design is insufficiently detailed
- you do not work as a team to develop the design.

Chapter 15 – Dreamweaver templates

This chapter will introduce you to **Dreamweaver MX 2004** and take you through the steps involved in creating a simple website. If you have an earlier or later version of **Dreamweaver**, most of the steps and screenshots are very similar.

Folder structure

When you set up a new site, you will be asked where on your computer you want it to be saved. It is therefore a good idea to create a suitable folder structure before opening a new site.

Each page on your site and each image you use will be a separate file. By the time you have created a website with many pages and images there will be a lot of files, so you need to make sure that they are well-organised from the start.

For any website, you will want four main folders – for **HTML** files, images, library and templates.

HTML files

Each page in your website will be an **HTML** file and will go in the **HTML** folder.

Images

Any image inserted on a web page is stored separately as an image file and should be put in the **Images** folder. The image files used in the **C3** website are all **JPEG** (**.jpg**) files; other common file types used for images are **.gif** and **.png**.

Library

The library is not actually used in this book but we will create the folder anyway because it is good practice.

When you are creating your website, you can add various objects such as images or paragraphs of text to the library. This is useful for items that are used often, because if a library item is updated, every instance of this library item on the website is also updated. Each item added to the library is given its own library file, which is stored in the **Library** folder.

Templates

As soon as you create a template, **Dreamweaver** will automatically create a **Templates** folder for you, so you won't need to create that yourself. You can create templates in **Dreamweaver** in much the same way as **Word**. Once the template is created, you can base subsequent pages on that template. All template files have the file extension **.dwt** and will be stored in the **Templates** folder.

Creating the folders

You can create the folders using the **Files** panel in **Dreamweaver**. However, if you are completely new to **Dreamweaver**, it may be advisable to use **Windows Explorer** because you will be more familiar with it, so we will use the **Files** panel later.

Using Windows Explorer

To create the folders in **Windows Explorer**:

 Open **Windows Explorer** by right-clicking on the **Start** button and clicking **Explore** from the menu that appears.

Figure 15.1: Opening Windows Explorer from the Start menu

 Find a suitable place to put the website folders – this will probably be somewhere in **My Documents**.

 Create a folder and name it **C3 Website**.

 Create three more folders in the **C3 Website** folder named **HTML_Files**, **Images** and **Library**. You don't need to create the **Templates** folder because **Dreamweaver** will create it for you when you save your first template.

 Your file structure should now look like this:

Figure 15.2: The file structure

 Close **Windows Explorer** and return to **Dreamweaver**.

Using the Files panel

 In **Dreamweaver**, click the **Files** panel in the **Files** panel group.

 Tip:

In version MX, the **Files** panel is called the **Site** panel.

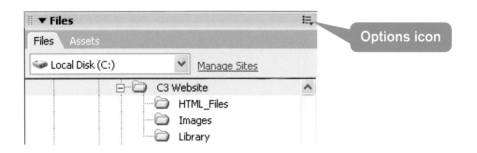

Figure 15.3: The Files panel

If you have already created your folders, you should be able to navigate to them in just the same way that you would within **Windows Explorer**. If you haven't created them yet, click the **Options** icon at the top right of the **Files** panel and then select **File** from the menu that appears. From this menu you can select to create a new folder.

Options icon

Creating a new site

 If the **Start** page is not visible, select **Site**, **Manage Sites** from the main menu bar.

 Note:

Select **New Site** from the **Site** menu in version MX.

 In the **Manage Sites** window, click the **New** button, then click **Site** on the small sub-menu that appears.

The **Site Definition** window appears. By default the **Basic** tab will be selected. This will take you through the **Wizard**. We will not use the **Wizard**, because it includes a lot of options that we just don't need at this stage.

 Click the **Advanced** tab.

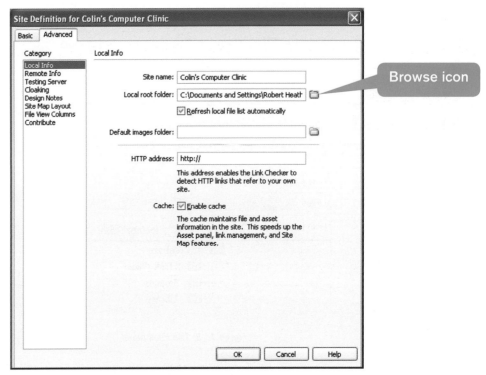

Figure 15.4: Site Definition window

Enter **Colin's Computer Clinic** as the **Site name**.

Browse icon

Click the **Browse** icon next to the **Local root folder** and locate the **C3 Website** folder that you just created.

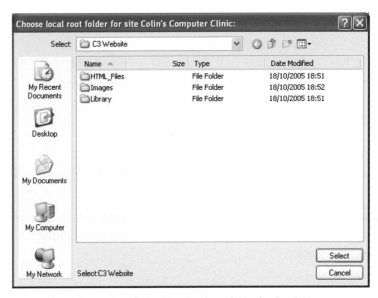

Figure 15.5: Selecting a local root folder for the site

 Click **Select**.

 You do not need to fill in any of the other options yet so just click **OK** and then **Done** in the **Manage Sites** window.

You have now set up the website ready to start adding web pages.

Tip:

In version MX, the workspace will open with a new blank page called **Untitled-1** already created. You can leave this open for now.

The Files panel

Note that all of the folders you have set up now appear in the **Files** panel. Anything associated with this site will be coloured green, as shown in Figure 15.6.

If your folders don't appear in the **Files** panel, make sure that you have **Colin's Computer Clinic** and **Local View** selected.

Figure 15.6: The Files panel

You can easily change folder names, add new folders or delete files using the **Files** panel in the same way as you would using **Windows Explorer**.

Basing a website on a template

All of the web pages for **Colin's Computer Clinic** will be based on a template, so that they all have the same design and layout.

The key to a really professional-looking website is to use a clean, simple template and to base every page on the same template. The navigation bar is also included on the template, so that whichever page you are on you have access to the same navigation buttons. This not only makes the website look professional and coherent, but it also makes it easy for people to browse your website without getting lost.

Downloading the image files

You will need to have several images for the website. These are available to download from **www.payne-gallway.co.uk**; click on the relevent link in the DiDA section.

Once you have found them make sure you download them into the **Images** folder of your website.

The **Files** panel of your site should now look like Figure 15.7.

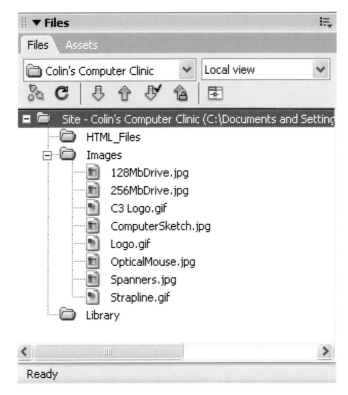

Figure 15.7: The Files panel after downloading the images

Creating a new template

You can create a template from scratch or an existing page can be converted into a template. We will create a basic page and then later save it as a template.

 Select **File**, **New** from the main menu bar.

The **New Document** dialogue box appears, as shown in Figure 15.8.

Figure 15.8: The New Document dialogue box

⊚ Click the **General** tab.

⊚ Make sure **Basic Page** is selected in the **Category** list and **HTML** from the second list. Click **Create**.

The new blank page appears, as shown in Figure 15.9.

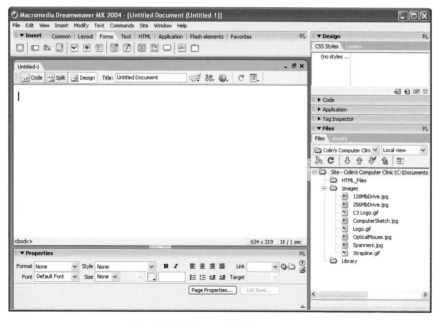

Figure 15.9: The new blank page appears

Tip:

You could create a template page by selecting **HTML template** from the **Basic page** list – see Figure 15.8. This would achieve the same result as saving the basic page as a template.

Saving a page as a template

You have now opened a new page but it is not yet saved. When a file is saved it will appear in the **Files** panel. We will save the page now as a template.

▶ Select **File**, **Save as Template** from the main menu bar; a dialogue box appears.

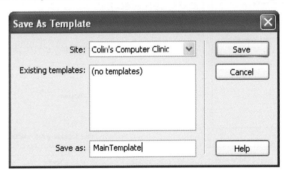

Figure 15.10: Saving a page as a template

▶ In the **Save as** field type **C3MainTemplate** and click **Save**.

The template may not yet be shown in the **Files** panel – you will need to refresh it first.

Refresh icon

▶ In the **Files** panel, click the **Refresh** icon.

Figure 15.11: The C3MainTemplate file appears in the Files panel

Note:

Although you didn't specify where **Dreamweaver** should save the file, it has automatically created a **Templates** folder and put it in there. If you had created the **Templates** folder along with the others, it would have found that and saved it in there.

In the next chapter we will finish creating the template.

Chapter 16 – Completing the template

Open **Dreamweaver** if it is not already open, and open **C3MainTemplate.dwt**.

Tables

You have probably come across tables in **Microsoft Word** which are used to store data in columns and rows. In **Dreamweaver** tables can also be used to store columns and rows of data but their main use is as a layout tool.

By using a large table, which is the size of the whole web page, you can adjust the columns and rows to divide up the page into sections.

A large table, which is the width of the whole page, will be the basis of our template.

The Insert bar

Whenever you want to insert anything, such as a table, an image or a navigation bar, etc., you will use the **Insert** bar. This is located at the top of the screen, just below the main menu bar.

Figure 16.1: The Insert bar, Show as Menu

There are two different views of the **Insert** bar. The one which appears when you first open **Dreamweaver** is **Show as Menu**, as shown in Figure 16.1 above. If yours looks like this, change it to **Show as Tabs**, as follows:

 Click where it says **Common** on the **Insert** bar, then select **Show as Tabs** from the menu that appears.

Figure 16.2: Selecting Show as Tabs

The **Insert** bar now appears as shown below.

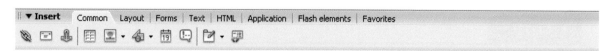

Figure 16.3: The Insert bar, Show as Tabs

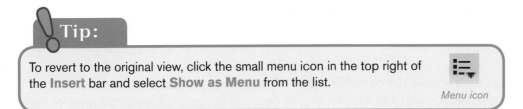

Chapter 16 – Completing the template

Tip:

To revert to the original view, click the small menu icon in the top right of the **Insert** bar and select **Show as Menu** from the list.

Menu icon

We'll leave the **Insert** bar in **Show as Tabs** view.

Inserting a table

⊙ Make sure that the cursor is in the top left of the page (it will be unless you have moved it), which is where we want to insert the table.

Table icon

⊙ Click the **Table** icon on the **Insert** bar (this is under the **Common** tab, which should already be selected). The **Table** dialogue box appears.

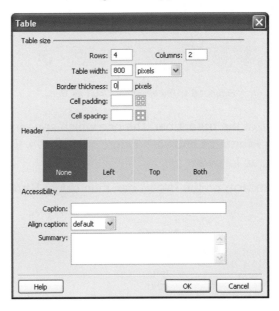

Figure 16.4: The Table dialogue box

⊙ Fill out the **Table** dialogue box as shown in Figure 16.4 above, with **4 Rows** and **2 Columns**. Enter the **width** as **800 pixels**. A value of **0** for the **Border thickness** gives an invisible border.

⊙ Click **OK**.

Tip:

Most sites use a width of about **800** pixels. At this size, each page of your site will fit onto most screens without users having to scroll across. Some sites are as narrow as **600** pixels – this means that even people with relatively small screens can view a page without scrolling, but you can't fit as much on a page. **www.payne-gallway.co.uk** uses a width of **600** pixels. **www.bbc.co.uk** uses just less than **800**.

The table appears as shown in Figure 16.5. It will need adjusting later on.

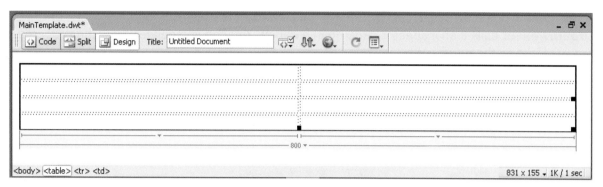

Figure 16.5: Inserting a new table

Selecting cells, rows and tables

The table in the screenshot above is selected – as yours probably is because you have only just created it. You can tell that it is selected because it has a solid black border and small black handles around it. It also has green lines and text indicating the width of the table in pixels.

▶ Click away from the table to deselect it. The handles and green lines will disappear.

▶ Now click in the middle of the table. Look at the text in the bottom left of the page:

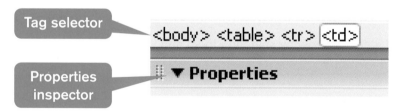

Figure 16.6: The Tag selector

These are called **Tags** and the area they are in is called the **Tag selector**. Clicking on them here will select the objects they represent.

▶ Clicking **<td>** will select the **cell** that the cursor is in.

▶ Clicking **<tr>** will select the **row** that the cursor is in.

▶ Clicking **<table>** will select the **table** that the cursor is in.

▶ Click each of these tags in turn and watch the black border highlight different parts of the table. This is the easiest way to select parts of a table.

137

The Properties inspector

At the bottom of the screen is the **Properties inspector** (it is essentially another panel, but **Dreamweaver** calls it an inspector rather than a panel). You can immediately view the properties of any object on the page just by selecting it.

 If you can't see the **Properties inspector**, select **Window**, **Properties** from the main menu bar. If the panel is collapsed, just click the small black arrow to the left of where it says **Properties**.

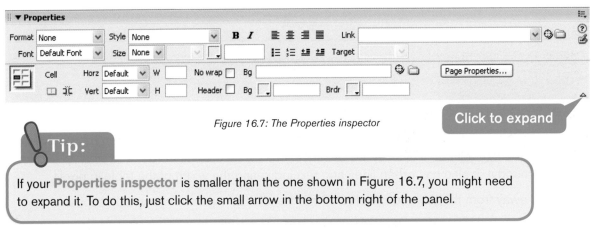

Figure 16.7: The Properties inspector

Click to expand

Tip:

If your **Properties inspector** is smaller than the one shown in Figure 16.7, you might need to expand it. To do this, just click the small arrow in the bottom right of the panel.

 Select the table you have just created by clicking the **<table>** tag.

The table properties appear in the **Properties inspector**. You will learn more about these later.

 Look at the properties of a cell and row by selecting them and viewing them in the **Properties inspector**.

Inserting and deleting rows and columns

Adding or deleting the last row or column

You can add or delete the bottom row or right-hand column simply by changing the number of rows and columns in the table properties (within the **Properties inspector**).

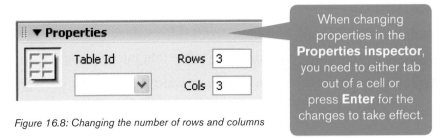

When changing properties in the **Properties inspector**, you need to either tab out of a cell or press **Enter** for the changes to take effect.

Figure 16.8: Changing the number of rows and columns

 Make sure that the table is selected. Change the number of **Rows** to **3** and **Columns** to **3**.

Tip:

Another way to add a row is to place the cursor in the last cell in a table and press the **Tab** key.

Inserting or deleting a row or column in the middle of a table

▶ Right-click in the top left cell in the table; a drop-down menu appears, as shown in Figure 16.9.

▶ Select **Table, Insert Row**.

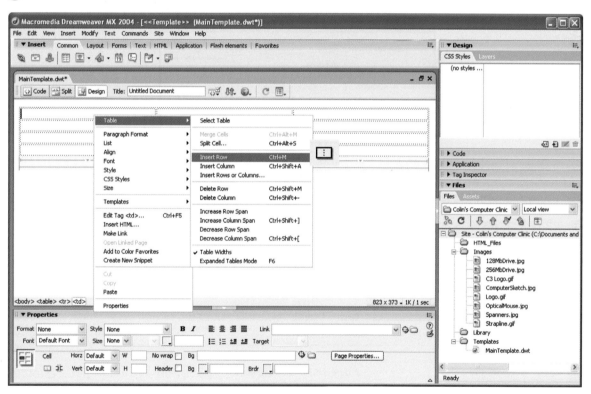

Figure 16.9: Inserting a row

The table should now have four rows and four columns.

Merging and splitting cells

You can easily merge and split cells so that the number of rows and columns varies across the table. The quickest way to merge and split cells is to use the icons in the **Properties inspector**.

Merging

▶ Select the entire second row in the table. Click the **Merge Cells** icon in the **Properties inspector**.

Merge Cells icon

The cells are merged and there is only one column in the second row.

139

▶ Merge the third and fourth cells in row **1**.

▶ Merge the third and fourth cells in row **3**.

Splitting

▶ Select the left cell in row **4**.

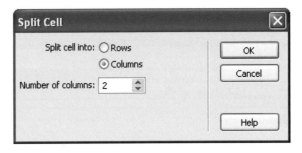

Split Cells icon

▶ Click the **Split Cells** icon in the **Properties** inspector.

The **Split Cell** dialogue box appears. You have the choice of splitting the cell into rows or columns. You can also specify how many rows or columns.

Figure 16.10: Splitting cells

▶ Enter the settings shown above then click **OK**.

The left cell in row 4 is split in two vertically, as shown in Figure 16.11.

Figure 16.11: Splitting cells

Resizing cells and tables

Resizing a table

The table should at least fill the visible area on the screen, so we need to make it much longer.

▶ Select the whole table. Place the mouse over the bottom handle so that it becomes a small double-headed arrow.

▶ Click and drag the handle down so that the table is about **600** pixels (the height will be shown in the **Properties inspector**). Release the mouse when you are happy with the size.

Tip:

You need not worry about a table cell being too small to fit an object in because the table will always grow to fit whatever you put in it.

Resizing cells

- To resize cells, just click and drag the table border between the cells.

- Place the mouse over the border you want to resize so that the cursor becomes an arrow.

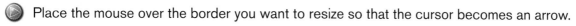
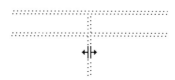

Figure 16.12: Resizing rows and columns

- Click and drag the border to where you want it, then release.

- Click and drag the borders so that your table looks like the one below. You will also need to add another cell using the **Split Cells** button. Resizing tables isn't an exact science in **Dreamweaver**; it sometimes takes a bit of trial and error – and a bit of patience!

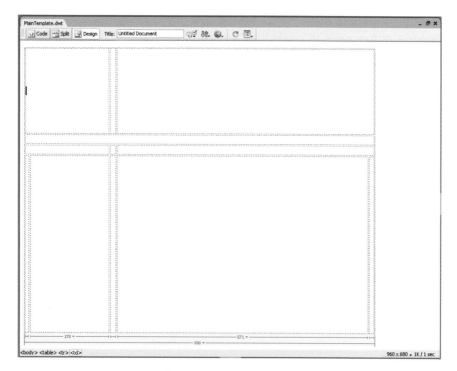

Figure 16.13: Resizing tables

Eliminating borders

For the look you want in this website you need to remove the white gaps between the cells.

▶ Make sure that the entire table is selected by clicking on the **<table>** tag.

▶ Set the **CellSpace** and **Border** properties to **0**, as shown in Figure 16.14.

Figure 16.14: Eliminating borders

Saving the template

It is very important to save your work regularly.

▶ To save the template simply click on **File**, **Save** on the main menu or press **Ctrl–S** for a shortcut.

▶ If you see a message concerning editable regions, click **OK**.

Inserting images

You need to insert the logo and strapline to the top row of the table. These images will then be visible on every page of the website since they are added to the main template.

▶ Click in the top left cell of the table.

Insert Image button

▶ Click the **Insert Image** button on the **Insert** bar. The **Select Image Source** window appears.

▶ Select the **Logo** image from the **Images** folder of your website, as shown in Figure 16.15.

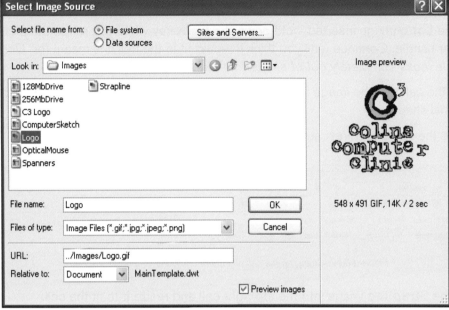

Figure 16.15: Inserting the logo image

 Click **OK**.

Accessibility

This refers to the practice of making web pages more readable to blind or partially sighted people. Special software can read out the text but images need to be described in words when the web page is created. You can specify **Alternate text**, which briefly describes the image and will be read out. The Alternative text window appears when you insert an image. You can also add alternate text in the Alt field of the **Properties Inspector** when an image is selected.

The **Alternate Text** appears when the cursor rolls over the image in a web browser.

Figure 16.16: Inserting alternate text

 **Tip:**

Accessibility is a feature that is specified in the mark scheme for the SPB and it will be obvious to the moderator if it has been done or not!

Resizing images

▶ With the **Logo** image inserted, hold down the **Shift** key while you resize the picture using a corner handle. Continue until you think it would fit in the cell it is meant for. *Don't worry if the table looks completely out of shape!*

▶ Select the cell that the image is in by clicking on the **<td>** tag. Your table should return to its normal shape.

▶ Change the **Horz** and **Vert** settings to **Center** and **Middle**.

Figure 16.17: Changing the cell alignment using the Properties inspector

▶ Insert the **Strapline** image into the top right cell and resize it to fit the cell.

▶ Enter appropriate **Alternate text** for the **Strapline** image.

▶ With the cell selected, set the **Horizontal** and **Vertical** alignment to **Center** and **Baseline**.

The top of the template should now appear as shown in Figure 16.8.

Figure 16.18: The top of the template so far

Changing the background colour

▶ Select the top row of the table by putting the cursor in one of the cells and clicking the **<tr>** tag.

▶ Select the drop-down box for the **Background Color Selector** marked **Bg** in the **Properties inspector** as shown in Figure 16.19.

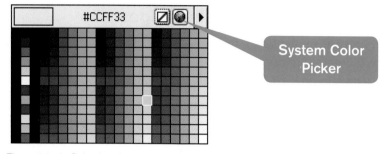

Figure 16.19: Selecting the background colour

The mouse cursor turns into a pipette. Use the **Color Dropper** by clicking inside the **3** of the **C3** logo to select the same colour.

Shade the other cells in similar colours to those shown in Figure 16.20 using the **System Color Picker**.

Figure 16.20: The template with background colour added

 Tip:

Colours chosen from the palette are **web safe**, meaning that they will look the same on any browser. A blend of colours on the other hand, such as from the **Colour Picker**, is not guaranteed.

Adding headings for other pages

The large cell on the left of the table will contain four headings that link to the other pages that you will create. Although you cannot actually hyperlink them yet, it is a good idea to put them into your template now so that you can see what it will look like when all the pages are put together.

⊳ Click in the large, pale green cell.

⊳ Type the heading **home** and press **Enter**.

⊳ Type in **products**, **services** and **contact us** underneath.

⊳ In the **Properties inspector**, have a look at the available fonts in the **Font** field. If you do not have the **Outwrite** font available, click on the **Edit Font List** option.

⊳ Click on the **Edit Font List** option at the bottom of the **Font** list, select the **Outwrite** font in the list of **Available fonts** and add it to your **Chosen fonts**. Click **OK**.

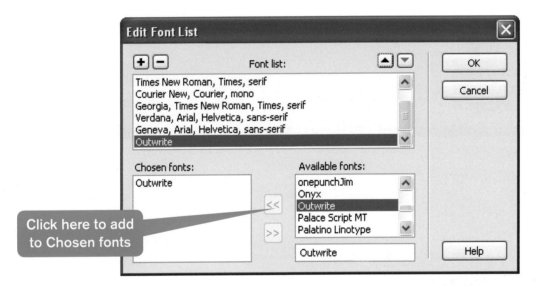

Figure 16.21: Adding fonts to your website

⊳ In the **Properties inspector**, you can now change the **Font** style to **Outwrite**, size **28 Pixels**.

⊳ Make the headings the same colour as the **Dark Green** bar underneath the images.

⊳ Position them at the **Top** of the cell using the **Vertical** alignment setting in the **Properties inspector**. Add a couple of extra lines so that they are not right at the top.

⊳ **Save** the template by pressing **Ctrl–S**.

Your template should now look like this:

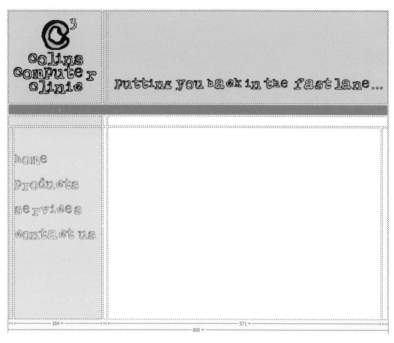

Figure 16.22: The template page

Editable regions

When you base other web pages on this template, any areas that have not been specified as editable regions will become locked. This means that you will not be able to change those areas that you have not specifically made editable.

You will need to define the large blank cell as an editable region so that the content can be added to each of the other web pages. To do this,

- Click in the large blank cell.
- In the **Insert** bar at the top of the screen, make sure that the **Common** tab is selected.

> **Note:**
>
> Select the **Templates** tab if you are using version MX.

- Click the drop-down arrow next to the **Templates** icon.

- Now click the **Editable Region** button. You are now asked to name the editable region.

Templates icon

- Call it **PageContent** and click **OK**.
- Set the **Vertical** alignment of the cell to **Top**.

The text **PageContent** now appears in the top left of the large blank cell, as shown in Figure 16.23.

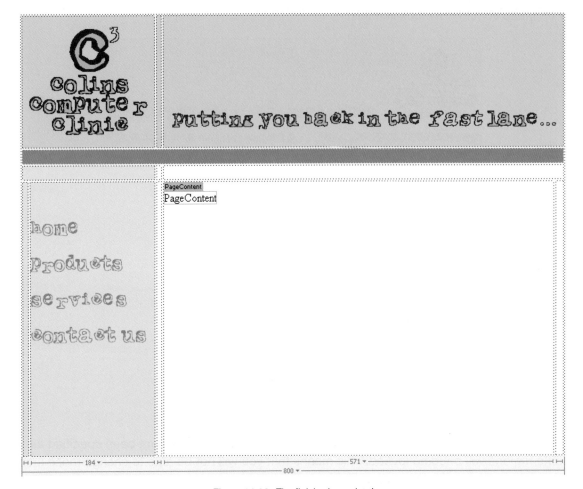

Figure 16.23: The finished template!

Save and Close the template file.

Chapter 17 – Creating the website

Now that you have created your template in **Dreamweaver**, you can use it to very quickly create all four of your company web pages. After that you can create hyperlinks to join them all up and form a proper website.

Opening a new web page

▶ Load **Dreamweaver MX 2004**.

▶ **Dreamweaver** may open with a new file called **Untitled-1**. If so, just close it without saving.

▶ Click **File**, **New**.

▶ Select the **Templates** tab. Notice that the window name has changed to **New from Template**.

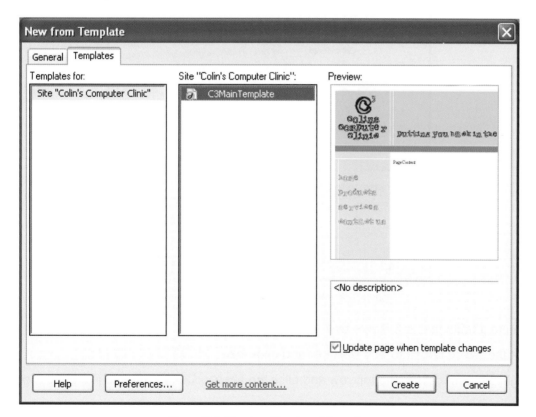

Figure 17.1: New from Template dialogue box

▶ Select **C3MainTemplate** for **Colin's Computer Clinic** that you made in the last chapter.

▶ Click **Create**.

▶ You should see a new page with the template design. Try changing a part of the template that you did not specify as editable. It will be locked.

Adding text

▶ Highlight the **PageContent** text with the white background and replace it with **Welcome to Colin's Computer Clinic.**

▶ Press **Enter.**

▶ Format the text as **Arial**, **18 Pixels**, **Bold** and **Dark Blue**, to match that used in the logo.

▶ Click the **Table** icon in the **Common** toolbar; the **Table** dialogue box appears.

Table icon

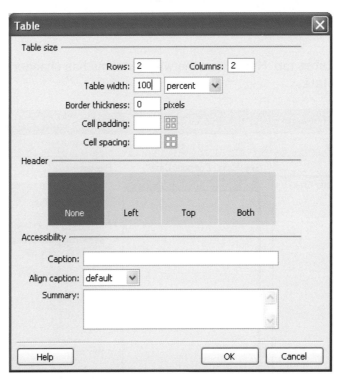

Figure 17.2: Inserting a table inside an editable region

▶ Create a table that is **2 Rows** by **2 Columns**.

▶ Set the **Table width** to **100 percent** and click **OK**.

Merge Cells button

▶ Highlight both cells in the top row and click the **Merge Cells** button to join them together.

Enter the text as shown in Figure 17.3. Format it as **Arial**, **14 pixels** and **Dark Blue**.

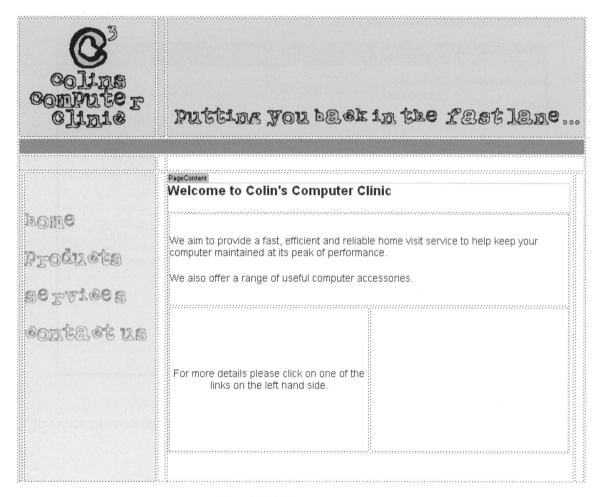

Figure 17.3: Adding text to your pages

Use the **Horz** and **Vert** positioning options to get the text where you want it.

Adding an image

Image button

▶ Click in the remaining blank cell and select the **Image** button on the **Common** toolbar. The **Select Image Source** dialogue box appears.

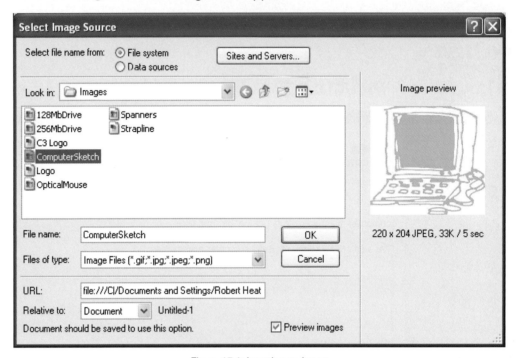

Figure 17.4: Inserting an image

▶ Select the **ComputerSketch** image that you should have saved in the **Images** folder of your website.

▶ Click **OK**, and **OK** again on any messages that may also pop up.

Saving your home page

Saving a home page is slightly different from saving a regular page. Firstly, it must be given a particular name, **index.html**. Secondly, it must be saved in the root folder of your website rather than in the **HTML_Files** folder. This is because nearly all servers look for a file called **index.html** in the root folder. If they can't find it, your website cannot be displayed.

▶ Click **File**, **Save**.

▶ In the **Save As** window enter the filename **index.html**, as shown in Figure 17.5.

> ### Note:
>
> It is important to remember the extension **.html** on the end of the filename. This makes it more likely to be accessible to other web browsers which may not recognise the default **.htm** extension.

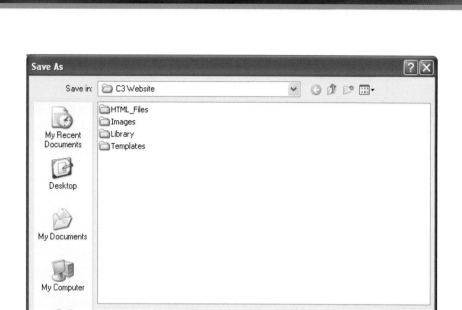

Figure 17.5: Saving the home page as index.html

▶ Click **Save**.

Previewing a web page

Now that you have saved your page you can try previewing it in a web browser such as **Internet Explorer**.

▶ If you have, **Internet Explorer** press the **F12** key.

▶ If you have a different browser, select **File**, **Preview in Browser** from the main menu. If the browser that you want to use isn't listed there, select **Edit Browser List**.

Tip:

Other browsers include **Firefox**, **Netscape** and **Opera**.

Naming your web page

In **Dreamweaver** you can specify the text that appears in the blue bar at the top of the web page window.

In the **Document** bar, name the page **C3 Home Page**.

Figure 17.6: Naming a web page

⊕ **Save** the page and view it again in a browser by pressing **F12**.

Figure 17.7: Previewing the page in a browser

Creating the Products page

⊕ Click on **File**, **New** on the main menu.

⊕ In the **New from Template** dialogue box select the **C3MainTemplate** and click **Create**.

⊕ Enter the heading **Products** and make it **Arial**, **18**, **Bold** and **Dark Blue**.

⊕ Add a table **8 Rows** by **4 Columns** at **100%**.

⊕ Recreate the rest of the web page shown in Figure 17.8, using the same styles that you used on the home page.

Figure 17.8: The Products page

It is very important to maintain the same styles for the headings and text throughout the entire site, to keep it looking professional.

You will need the two **USB flash memory stick** images and the **Optical Mouse** image to add to the table.

Name the page **C3 Products** and save it as **Products.html** in the **HTML_Files** folder of your website.

You should now see your **Products.html** file appear in the **Files** panel along with your index, template and image files.

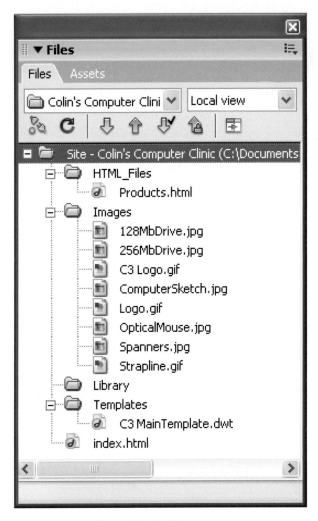

Figure 17.9: The Files window

The Services page

Create the **Services** page, as shown in Figure 17.10. Start by typing in the heading **Services** and then creating a table **3 Rows** by **2 Columns** at **100%**.

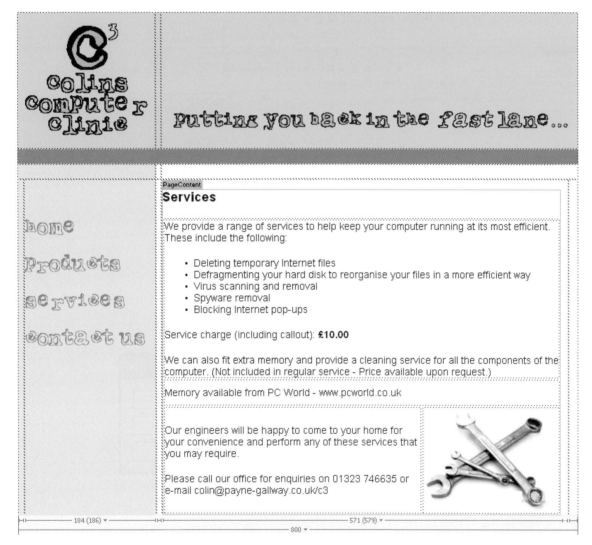

Figure 17.10: The Services page

There are two hyperlinks on this page which will be added later in this chapter.

Name the page **C3 Services** and save it in the **HTML_Files** folder as **Services.html**.

Adding a hyperlink to an external website

◉ Highlight the web address for PC World – **www.pcworld.co.uk**

◉ Type **http://www.pcworld.co.uk** in the **Link** box in the **Properties inspector**. It is important to type the **http://** in front of the link.

Figure 17.11: Adding a hyperlink to an external site

◉ Set the **Target** box to **_blank**. This will make the PC World website open in a new window.

◉ **Save** the page.

◉ Press **F12** to test your link in **Internet Explorer**.

Creating an e-mail hyperlink

◉ Highlight the text **colin@payne-gallway.co.uk/c3**.

◉ Click the **E-mail Link** button on the **Common** toolbar.

E-mail link button

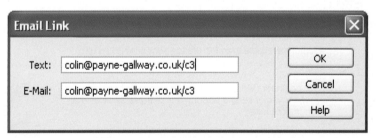

Figure 17.12: Creating an e-mail link

◉ Complete the **E-mail Link** window, as shown in Figure 17.12.

◉ Click **OK**.

The text should now be displayed with a blue underline. This is the standard way of displaying a hyperlink.

◉ **Save** and **Close** the **Services** page.

Creating the Contacts page

- Create a new page using the **C3MainTemplate**.
- Start by typing in the heading **Contact Us** and then adding a table **13 Rows** by **2 Columns** at **100%**.
- Complete the page, as shown in Figure 17.13, remembering to add the e-mail link.

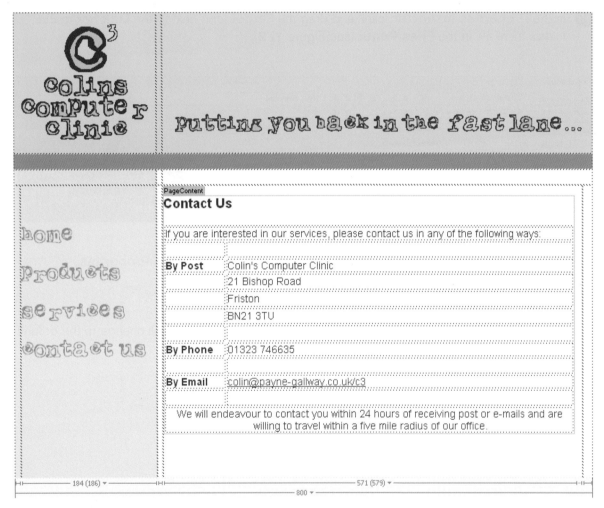

Figure 17.13: The Contacts page

- Save the **Contacts** page as **Contacts.html**.

Creating the hyperlinks on the main template

Now that you have created the individual web pages, you can create the hyperlinks that are going to connect the pages.

▶ Open the **C3MainTemplate.dwt** file by double-clicking it in the **Files Panel** on the right hand side of the page.

▶ Highlight the **Home** text in the navigation bar on the left.

▶ In the **Properties inspector**, click and drag the **Target** icon next to the **Link** box to the **index.html** file in the **Files Panel** (see Figure 17.9).

Target icon

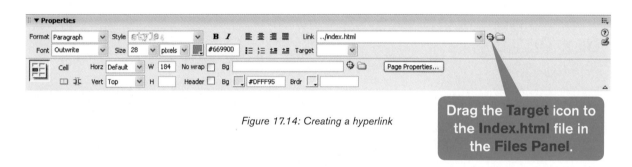

Figure 17.14: Creating a hyperlink

Drag the **Target** icon to the **Index.html** file in the **Files Panel**.

▶ You should find that **../index.html** will appear in the **Link** box on the **Properties inspector**, as shown in Figure 17.14.

▶ Repeat the operation for each of the other three links.

▶ You may need to re-format the colours of the hyperlinks since they will change to the default blue colour.

Updating pages that use the Main Template

Now that you have changed the main template, you need to make sure that each of the four files that use it are updated with the new working hyperlinks on their navigation bars. Because you used a template for each of them you can do this automatically.

Click on **File**, **Save** to save the **C3MainTemplate** file.

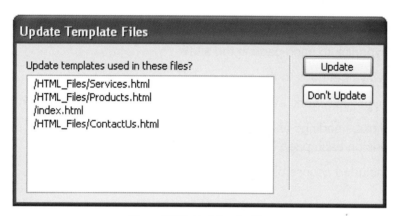

Figure 17.15: Updating the files

You will be asked if you want to update the templates used in the files listed. Click **Update**.

Now click **Close** in the **Update Pages** window.

Preview your website

If any of your web pages are already open, save them now to save the new hyperlinks.

Make sure that one of your web pages is open in **Dreamweaver** and press the **F12** key.

Try clicking on the links in your Browser.

Getting feedback

An important aspect of your project work is getting feedback from your group and other reviewers, then making changes and improvements when you agree with the comments.

If you are working as a group, you will probably decide on the basic format and layout of the template together. You could then each create a template on the computer and discuss these at your next meeting. It may also be worth asking an impartial reviewer for his or her feedback. The template that best suits your business can then be used by each group member as the one for the final website.

When the pages have all been designed, feedback should again be sought.

Testing the website

Every aspect of this entire project, including spreadsheets, presentations and websites, must be thoroughly tested. This is particularly important for the website and the eportfolio. If the moderator cannot, for example, link to a page containing your presentation, you will receive no marks for that element.

The following aspects need to be tested for every page.

- Is the spelling and grammar correct on every page?
- Is there a hyperlink to each page in the site?
- Can you always get back to the home page?
- Do all the hyperlinks work, even when viewed on a different computer?
- Are all the links, headings and standard elements such as the logo in consistent styles and positions on each page?
- Have you included accessibility features on each image?

Performing the tests

It is a good idea to go through every page with the list above and make a new list of very specific items that need to be tested. Make a note of every item that needs testing and tick it when you have tested it.

When you think that you have finished testing it properly, get someone else to test it!

Figure 17.6: Making a note of your tests

Good Marks... ✓

You will get good marks if you:

- create a storyboard for your website

- agree with your team who will do what and recorded it in your diary

- update your project plan.

Bad Marks... ✗

You will lose marks if:

- your website is incomplete

- your website contains any errors or inactive links.

Chapter 18 – Designing the eportfolio

By this stage you should have completed all the elements needed to put in the eportfolio, although some of them will still need to be put into the correct file format.

Creating a checklist

It is a very good idea to go through the SPB and look at every element of it carefully. It will tell you exactly what needs to go in the eportfolio and in which formats. Writing down everything you need to include is not only a good way to help you remember what you have created but also provides the basis for your menu structure or navigation bar in your eportfolio website.

 Look through the SPB and write a list of all the elements you need to include, and in what format.

Element	Format
Initial project plan	PDF or Text
Final annotated and amended plan	PDF or Text
Project diary	PDF or Text
Mind Map	JPEG
Market Research questionnaire	PDF or Text
Spreadsheet of financial analysis	JPEG of normal and formula views
Proposal presentation	PPS
Letterhead and business card	PDF or JPEG
Poster and Flyer	PDF or JPEG
Website and website storyboard	JPEG and hyperlink to index.html
Review	PDF or Text
Acknowledgements	Text

Figure 18.1: List of elements required by SPB

The greater your understanding of what is required in the eportfolio, the easier it will be to design and put together.

Preparing JPEG files

Several elements required for your eportfolio are not currently in the correct file format. For example, the SPB specifies that you should not include the actual spreadsheet. You could take a screenshot of it, and then reduce the file size in a graphics package such as **Photoshop Elements**. You can do this as follows.

- Load your spreadsheet **CashflowForecastV3.xls**.
- Scroll down the spreadsheet so that you can see the graph, cash flow forecast and profit and loss statement.

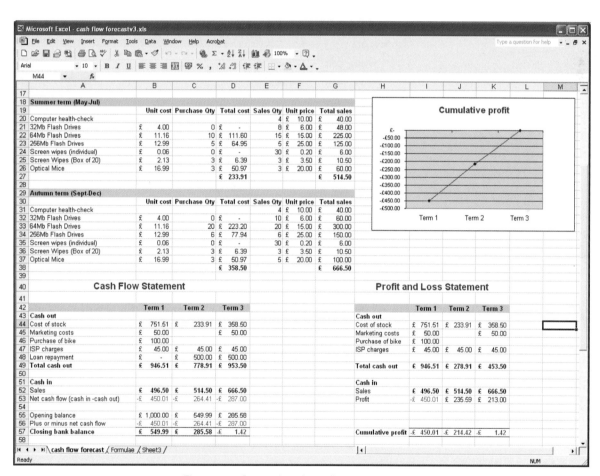

Figure 18.2: Screenshot of a profit and loss statement

- Press **Alt–Prt Scr** to capture a screenshot of the window.
- Open **Photoshop Elements** and from the **File** menu select **New From Clipboard**.
- Select **File**, **Save for Web**. A window will appear showing options.

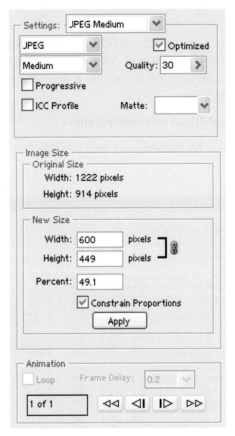

Figure 18.3: Compression options

▶ Set the **Width** to **600 pixels** so that it will approximately fit the area of the eportfolio web page it is destined for. In **Settings** set resolution to either **JPEG Medium** or **JPEG Low**.

▶ Click on **Apply**.

▶ **Save** it in the **Images** folder of the eportfolio.

▶ You can also save the original screen capture in **Photoshop** – do this and you can compare the file sizes. It will be at least four times the size of the compressed image.

Displaying the formulae in a spreadsheet

▶ You will need to repeat this operation to get an image of the spreadsheet formulae.

To display the formulae in your spreadsheet, click on **Tools**, **Options** and check the **Show Formulae** box. As a shortcut you can also press **Ctrl** + ¦ (the button next to the **1** key in the top left of your keyboard).

Creating an Adobe PDF file

Files created in **Word** or **Publisher** can easily be converted into **PDF** files. **PDF** stands for **Portable Document Format**, which means that the converted files can be read by anyone, even people that don't have the piece of software that the file were originally created in. You will need to have **Adobe Acrobat** installed to be able to do this.

You need to convert the poster and flyer into two separate **PDF** files.

- Open **Windows Explorer** and select the **C3Poster** file.
- Right-click the file and select **Convert to Adobe PDF**.

If you do not get this option on the shortcut menu, do the following instead:

- Double-click the **C3Poster** file in **Windows Explorer** to load the poster in **Publisher**.
- Select **File**, **Print**.
- In the **Print** dialogue box set the **Printer Name** to **Acrobat Distiller**.
- Click the **Properties** button and select the **Adobe PDF Settings** tab. Select **eBook** in the **Conversion Settings** and click **OK** twice.

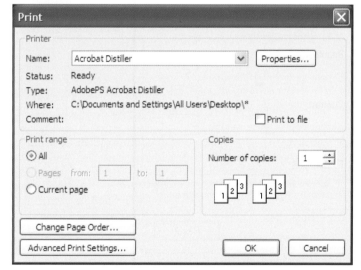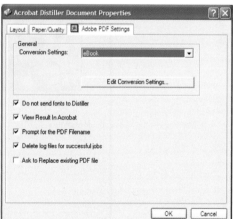

Figure 18.4: Creating a PDF file

- **Save** the file in the **Eportfolio** folder.
- Repeat the operation for anything else that needs to be in **PDF** format.

Scanning a document

Some elements required for your eportfolio are sketches on paper. For example, the SPB specifies that you should include the storyboard for your eportfolio. You will need to use a scanner to convert this page into a digital file format.

- Make sure that your computer has a scanner attached and switched on.
- Position the drawing carefully on the scanner and close the lid.
- Load **Photoshop Elements**.
- Click **Connect to Camera or Scanner** in the **Welcome** screen or **File**, **Import** from the main menu.
- Select the name of your scanner in the **Import** options list.
- Click **Custom Settings** and then **Adjust the quality of the scanned image**.
- In the **Advanced Properties** window, set the **Resolution** to a minimum of **75dpi** and select **Color picture**.

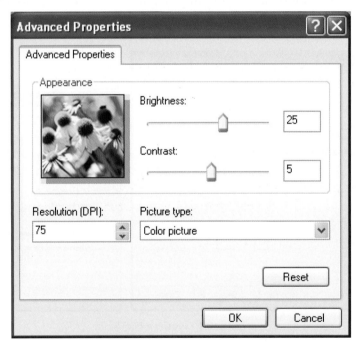

Figure 18.5: Adjusting the resolution of a scanned image

- Click **OK** and then **Preview** to begin scanning a preview of the image.
- Once it has displayed a rough image on the screen of your sketch, adjust the boundaries of the scan in the **Preview** window and click **Scan**.
- Your sketch will appear as an image in **Photoshop Elements**. **Rotate** it if necessary.
- Click **File**, **Save for web** and select **JPEG Medium** (see Figure 18.3).
- Save it as **Storyboard.jpg**.

Creating a structure chart

A structure chart shows how each element of the eportfolio will link together, in a similar way to how **Windows Explorer** displays your files and folders.

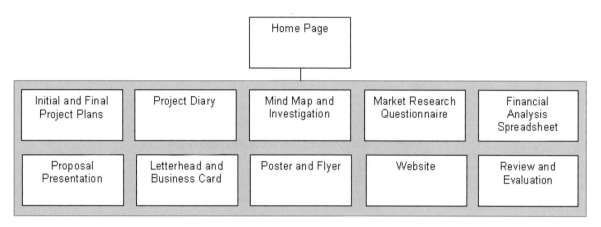

Figure 18.6: Creating a structure chart

 Use your checklist to create a structure chart of how each page will link together. In the chart above, each of the pages links to every other page.

Designing the layout of the eportfolio pages

The eportfolio will essentially be another website created in a very similar fashion to the promotional website you created using **Dreamweaver** for **Colin's Computer Clinic**. You will design a better website if you first sketch some ideas on paper – as shown in Figure 18.7. Ideally the eportfolio needs to be uncluttered and very easy for the examiner to navigate around.

> **Note:**
>
> The only person who is going to use your eportfolio is the moderator. Design it specifically for him or her!

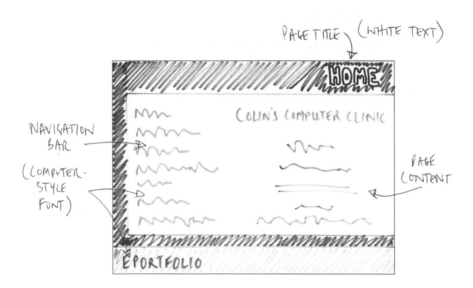

Figure 18.7: Draft layout sketch

Creating your design in Dreamweaver

In exactly the same way as you created the website for **Colin's Computer Clinic**, you need to set up the file structure first. You can do this in **Dreamweaver** using the **Files** panel or in **Windows Explorer**.

> The following steps will assume you already have some knowledge of **Dreamweaver** from creating the C3 website in earlier chapters. If you get stuck, look back through the book to see how things were done in the other website (pages 127–163).

Whichever method you choose to create your folders, open **Dreamweaver** and click on **Site**, **Manage Sites** to create a folder structure like the one shown in Figure 18.8.

Figure 18.8: Creating the folder structure

Creating the web page template

All websites are best produced using a template. This allows you to make sure that all pages look and are laid out the same, and cuts the amount of work that you need to do dramatically!

▶ On the main menu, click **File**, **New**.

▶ In the **New Document** dialogue box, with the **General** tab selected, click on **Category: Basic page**.

▶ Then select **HTML template** from the second list of options and click **Create**.

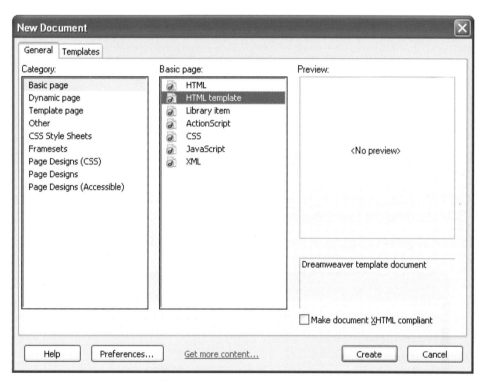

Figure 18.9: Creating a template page

Creating the structure with a table

▶ Using the **Table** button on the **Common** toolbar, create a table **6** rows by **6** columns.

▶ In the **Properties** window, set the **Table Width** to **800 Pixels**.

▶ Adjust the dimensions of the cells and use the **Merge** tool to set up the table like the one in Figure 18.10.

Table button

Figure 18.10: Creating a table structure

- Set the **Background Colour** properties for each of the cells where applicable.
- Add the headings for each of the other pages in the eportfolio. Note that all the headings are in a single cell.
- Select all the headings and set the text properties to **OCR A Extended**, size **Large** in **Dark Blue**. Select a different font if that one is not available to you.
- Set the **Vert** alignment setting in the **Properties** panel to **Top**.

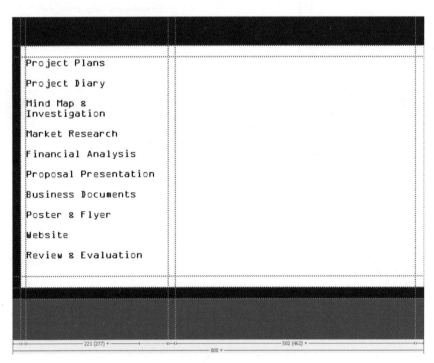

Figure 18.11: Adding table properties

Defining Editable Regions

- Select the large cell at the top right of the table and click the **Editable Regions** button in the **Common** toolbar.

- Name the region **PageTitle**.

- Select the cell and set the text properties to **OCR A Extended**, **XX-Large**, **White**, **Bold**.

- Set **Horz** and **Vert** alignment to **Right** and **Middle**.

- Define two more **Editable Regions**, as shown in Figure 18.12.

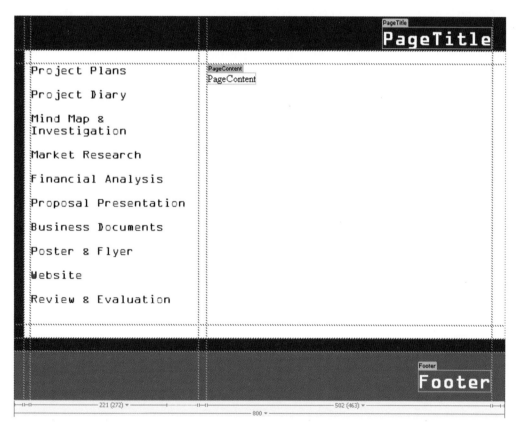

Figure 18.12: Adding editable regions

- In the **PageContent** region set **Vert** alignment to **Top**.

- Set the font style of the **Footer** region to **OCR A Extended**, **XX-Large**, **White** and **Bold**. Set **Horz** alignment to **Right** and **Vert** alignment to **Middle**.

- **Save** the template in the **Templates** folder of your site and call it **MainTemplate**.

Changing the link styles

This will set the colour of the link once visited, when the mouse hovers over it and when active.

⊙ Click the **Page Properties** button in the **Properties inspector**.

⊙ Select the **Links** category and change the settings to those shown in Figure 18.13.

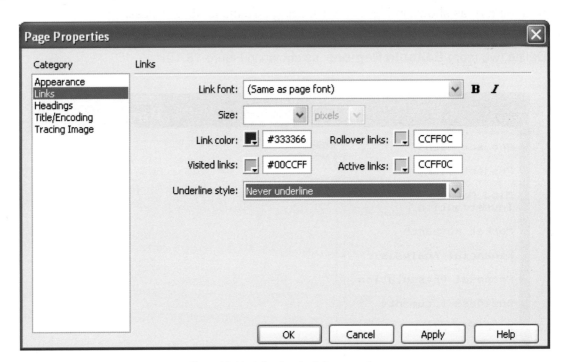

Figure 18.13: Adjusting the links properties

⊙ Click **Apply** and **OK**.

⊙ **Save** the template.

Creating the home page

The home page will be based on the template that you just created.

- From the main menu select **File**, **New** and open a new page based on **MainTemplate**.
- Add the title **Home** to the **PageTitle** area.
- Add the text, as shown in Figure 18.14, using suitable fonts and sizes.
- Centre the text using the **Center** button in the **Properties inspector**.
- **Delete** the text in **Footer** to leave this space blank.

Center button

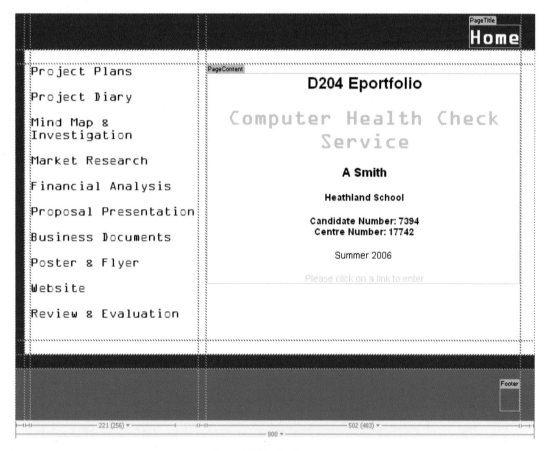

Figure 18.14: The home page

- **Save** the page in the main **Eportfolio** folder of the website as **Index.html**.
- Test the page in **Internet Explorer** by pressing the **F12** key.

In the next chapter we will create the rest of the pages.

Now that you have created the main template and home page for the eportfolio, you can begin creating each of the pages that form the rest of the site. You should already have learnt most of the skills needed to produce a new page.

Creating a new web page based on your template

Make sure that you have **Dreamweaver** open with the eportfolio selected as the current website that you are working on. If the folder structure for the eportfolio is not the current one shown in the **Files** panel, select it using the browser box.

This new page will be the **Project Plans** page.

- Select **File**, **New** on the main menu.

- In the **New from Template window**, click on the **D204 Eportfolio** site then click **Create**.

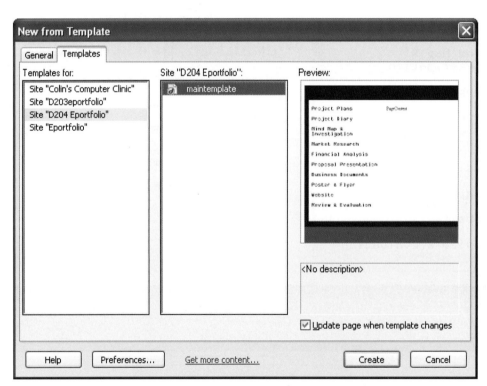

Figure 19.1: New from Template dialogue box

- Change the title of the page to **Project Plans** and alter the **Footer** to say **Home**.

- Enter the text as shown in Figure 19.2. Format it using a suitable font.

- Make **PDF** files of both project plans (original and final) and **Save** them in the **Eportfolio** folder.

- Make the word **HERE** a link to the **PDF** file using the **Point to file** button.

Point to File button

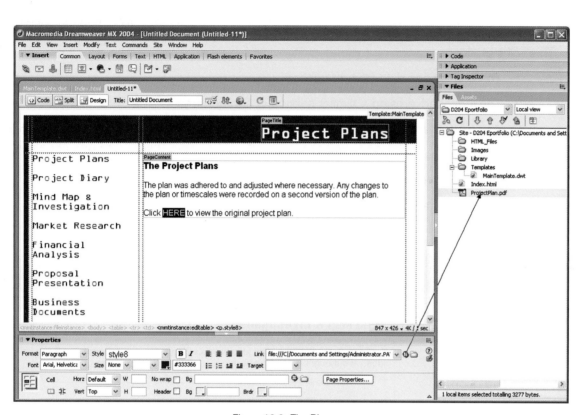

Figure 19.2: The Plan page

▶ **Save** the page in the **HTML_Files** folder as **Plans.html**.

Creating the Project Diary page

▶ Create this page in a very similar way to the **Project Plans** page.

Creating the Investigation page

The **Mind Map and Investigation** page will need to include (amongst other things) the Mind Map that you created earlier in this book. If you used **OpenMind** to make it, you can export the final Mind Map as a **JPEG** image. Chapter 3 explains how to do this (pages 12, 21).

▶ Make sure that the **Mind Map** image file has been saved for the web at a medium or low resolution in the **Images** folder of the eportfolio website.

▶ Create a page for the **Mind Map and Investigation** page.

▶ Add the title and text, then insert the **Mind Map** image into the **PageContent** area of the web page.

177

You will also need to insert the other pieces of data that you collected during your research. This will include:

1. The admissions data from the school.

2. The leaflet advertising a similar service in another area.

3. Any related articles collected from magazines or newspapers.

4. Web research into wholesale prices and availability of goods for sale.

5. Research into the retail prices of major stores.

Make sure that you have saved any images at a suitable resolution and put them in the **Images** folder.

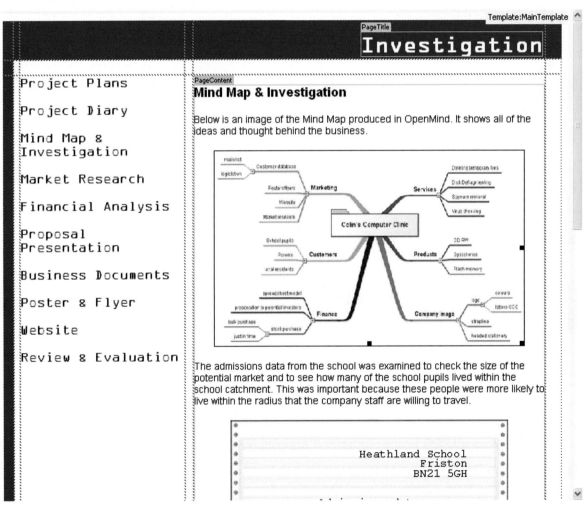

Figure 19.3: The Mind Map and Investigation page

Creating the Market Research page

The **Research** page is created in the same way as the previous page but this time the market research questionnaire is included. You could do this in one of three ways.

1. Take a screenshot of the questionnaire page by pressing **Prt Scr** and use a graphics package such as **Photoshop Elements** to save it for the web.

2. Use a specialised screen capture program.

3. Insert a link to a **PDF** document containing the questionnaire.

Figure 19.4 was created by inserting an image file of the questionnaire taken by a screen capture program.

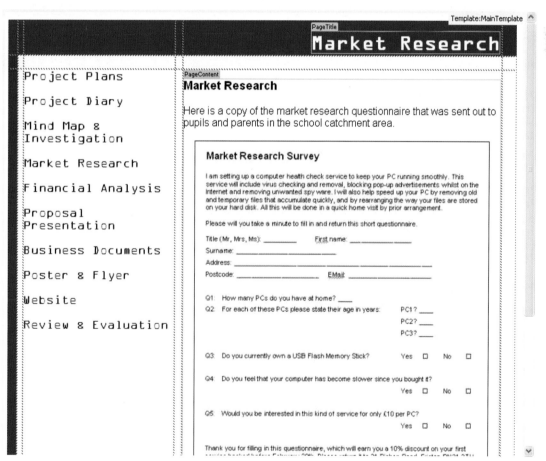

Figure 19.4: The Market Research page

Add some text at the bottom of the page explaining how many you sent out and the response that you received back.

Creating the Financial Analysis page

The **Financial Analysis** page needs to include evidence of the spreadsheet that you created to assess the potential profits of the company. You need to show evidence of the spreadsheet displaying your projected revenue and profits, your break-even analysis, some sensitivity analysis and the formulae you used in creating it. You should not include the spreadsheet itself.

You can show the potential profits, break-even and sensitivity analysis by copying and pasting some of the graphs that you produced. Also show the spreadsheet in **Formula** view.

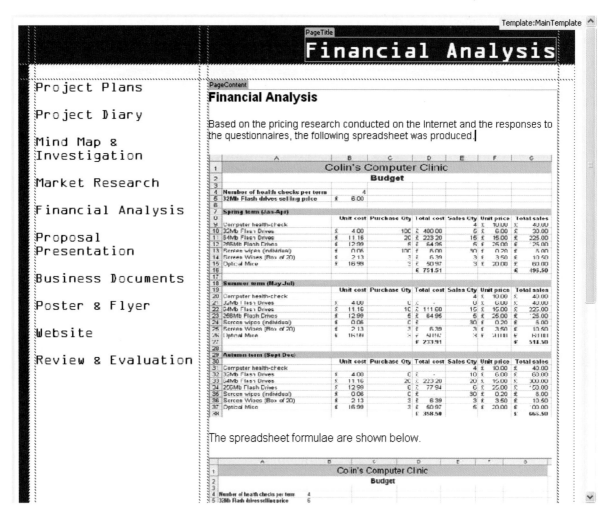

Figure 19.5: The Financial Analysis page

Creating a self-running PowerPoint presentation

In order for the presentation to be viewed without **PowerPoint** you need to save it as a show.

- With the **BusinessProposal** file still loaded, click on **File**, **Save As**.

- **Save** the file as **BusinessProposal** and select **PowerPoint Show** in the **Save as type** box.

- **Save** it in the **Eportfolio** folder.

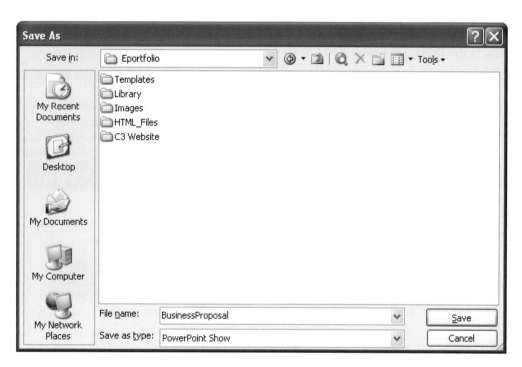

Figure 19.6: Saving as a PowerPoint Show

Creating the Proposal Presentation page

For the **Proposal Presentation** page, you will need to take a screenshot of the first page of the presentation. You can add this to the proposal page of the website and then use it as the hyperlink to the actual presentation.

- Load the **BusinessProposal** file.
- Take a screenshot of the first page and save it as a **JPEG** image.
- Insert the image into the web page.

You can also download the screenshot image from **www.payne-gallway.co.uk**; click on the relevant link in the DiDA section.

- **Hyperlink** the image to the **BusinessProposal.pps** file in the **Eportfolio** folder.
- Set the **Target** to **_blank** in the **Properties** panel. This will open the **PowerPoint** file in a new window, allowing the moderator to go back to the eportfolio more easily.

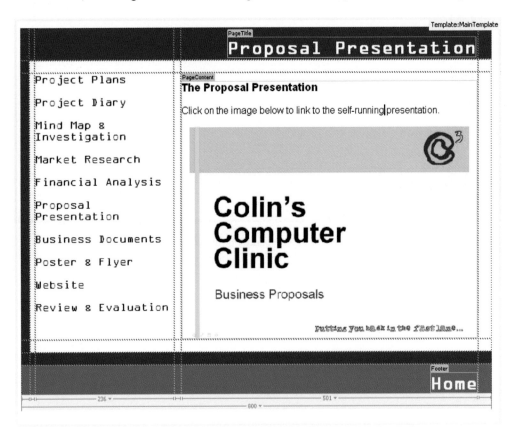

Figure 19.7: The Proposal Presentation page

Creating the Business Documents page

For this page you should include your business card, the letterhead template and the invoice template. Either add them as **PDF** files or take a screenshot of them and save the image file in the **Images** folder of your website.

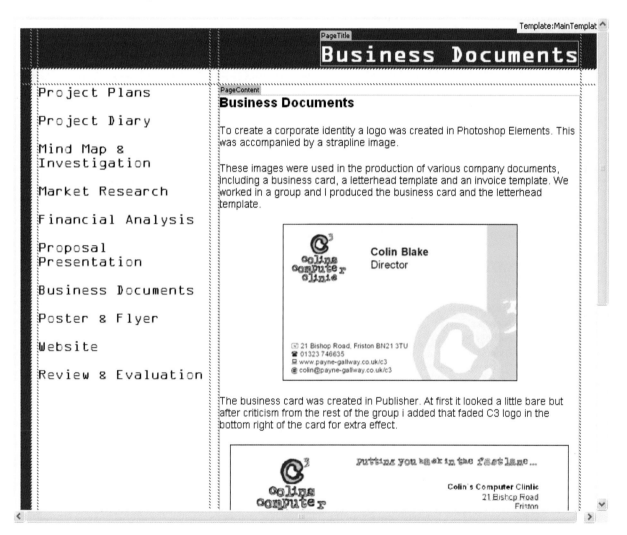

Figure 19.8: The Business Documents page

The Poster and Flyer page

The **Poster and Flyer** page would be best viewed as **PDF** documents. You can convert the posters you have made into **PDF** files and then link thumbnail images of the posters on the web page to the real ones.

Managing your files

You need to make a hyperlink from your eportfolio to the website you made earlier in the book. To do this, you need to move your **C3 Website** files into the root folder for the eportfolio, called **Eportfolio**.

Use **Windows Explorer** to move the website files into the **Eportfolio** folder, exactly as shown in Figure 19.9.

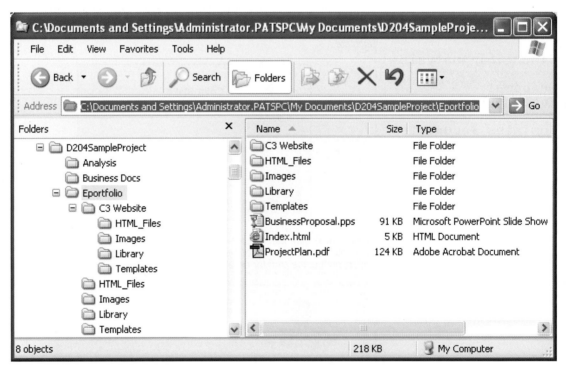

Figure 19.9: Moving your C3 Website files into the Eportfolio root folder

The Website page

The first thing that you need to include in the **Website page** is a scanned image of the storyboard that you sketched out when you were designing the website.

Tip:

Remember to set the scanner resolution to 150dpi and then use a graphics package to reduce the resolution down to 72dpi for the best quality.

- **Open** a new page and **Insert** text, as shown in Figure 19.10.
- **Insert** the scanned storyboard.
- **Insert** a screenshot (at **72dpi**) of the **C3 website** home page. This will become the hyperlink to the **C3 website**.

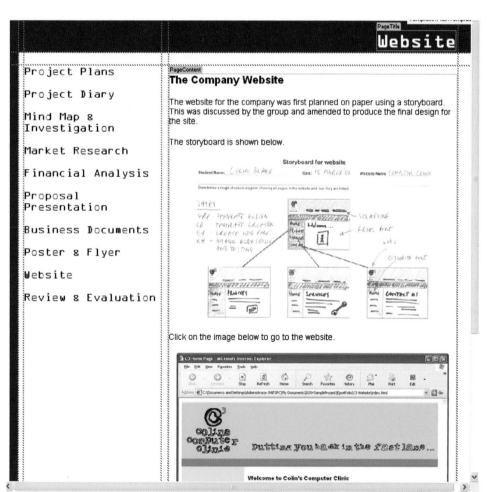

Figure 19.10: The Website page

Inserting a hyperlink

Now you can add a hyperlink to link the image to the home page of the **C3 website**.

 Click on the **Home page** image to select it.

 In the **Properties inspector**, drag the **Point to File** target by the **Link** box over to the **index.html** file of the **C3 Website**. The filename and path should appear in the box.

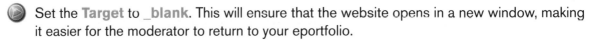 Set the **Target** to **_blank**. This will ensure that the website opens in a new window, making it easier for the moderator to return to your eportfolio.

Point to File target

Figure 19.11: Creating a hyperlink

 **Save** the web page as **Website.html** and test out the hyperlink by pressing **F12**.

Review and Evaluation page

 Create a new page for the **Review** and **Evaluation**.

 Change the **PageTitle** to **Review & Evaluation** and the **Footer** to **Home**.

 Leave the rest blank and **Save** the page as **Review.html**.

As well as the review of each element you have created for this project, you will also need to get your eportfolio reviewed by your teacher and your peers before you can complete this page. You can read the advice given in the next chapter before you start.

Linking the pages together

With all the pages in the site complete, you can now start to link all of them together. This is done in the same way that you used to create hyperlinks earlier (page 160), except that you can now add the hyperlinks to the headings in the navigation bar of the **MainTemplate**.

 Double-click on the **MainTemplate** file in the **Files** panel to open it.

 Highlight the first heading, **Project Plans**.

▶ Use the **Point to File** icon in the **Properties inspector** next to the **Links** box and drag the target over to the **Plans.html** file in the **Files** window.

Point to File target

▶ Repeat the operation for the rest of the links.

▶ Save the **MainTemplate** file. Click **Update** in the window that appears. This will update all the other **html** files that use the template you have just modified.

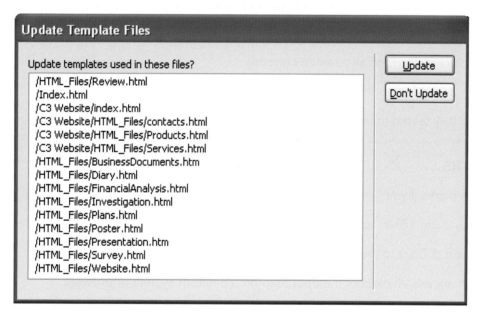

Figure 19.12: Updating pages based on the MainTemplate

▶ Open the **Index.html** file and press **F12** to test your new site.

You will notice that all of the links on the left-hand side should work and that the **C3 Website** opens in a new window. You still need to link up the **Home** link in the bottom right of each page.

▶ Open each of the **html** files in turn and link them all to the **Index.html** page of the **D204 Eportfolio** site.

Chapter 19 – Creating the eportfolio

Good Marks... ✓

You will get good marks if you:

- make sure that all your files are in acceptable file formats
- have included everything required and nothing unnecessary
- have made all the links and text consistent styles and positions
- have included accessibility features
- have acknowledged all sources correctly
- have asked for feedback and made use of it
- have fully tested the eportfolio.

Bad Marks... ✗

You will lose marks if you:

- go over the 18Mb size limit
- make it difficult to navigate
- can't access all parts of the eportfolio on a different system or browser
- forget to put all of your candidate and centre details on the home page.

Chapter 20 – Review and evaluation

When reviewing your coursework you need to make sure that you consider each of the following:

- the project as a whole
- each element of the project included in your eportfolio, including the eportfolio itself
- your own performance.

Tip:

You will find the syllabus materials on the Internet very helpful for this section. They are easy to understand and well set out. Go to Edexcel's **DiDA SPB204** website and click on the **Review** section.

In this module there is a lot of emphasis on working in a team. While working through this book, hopefully you have had some opportunities to work in a team and will have discovered some of the pitfalls as well as the advantages. Think about how well you worked as a team. If you have a weak team member for your next project, you are going to have to find ways of working with this person or making the most of his or her work. One of the things that you can put in your review is what you did if someone was away or did not do their share of the work. This is an important life skill!

Including feedback on each element

Each element of your eportfolio needs to be reviewed. It is best to show some examples of early ideas, feedback on these ideas, final designs reflecting your feedback, and even some feedback on the final designs.

As an example, the initial design of the C3 poster is shown in Figure 20.1 and reviewed in an e-mail in Figure 20.2.

The review and the initial design should be shown in the review section of the eportfolio, along with the final design once the reviewer's comments have been implemented.

'… in order to improve the poster, you need to remove the hyphenation and add some more text to the bottom half of it' and *'… centralise it a bit more'*.

Figure 20.1: The initial design of the C3 Poster

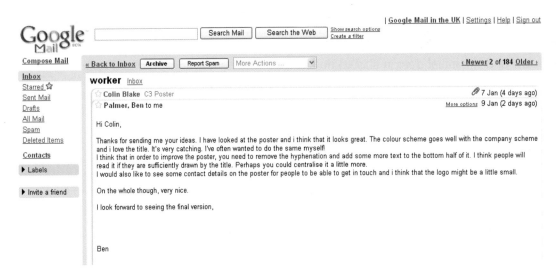

Figure 20.2: Feedback on the C3 Poster

The reviewer also added that there should be *'…some contact details on the poster'… 'and that the logo might be a little small'*.

Once you have shown your feedback on the first draft, you can show your final draft, displaying any final feedback after that.

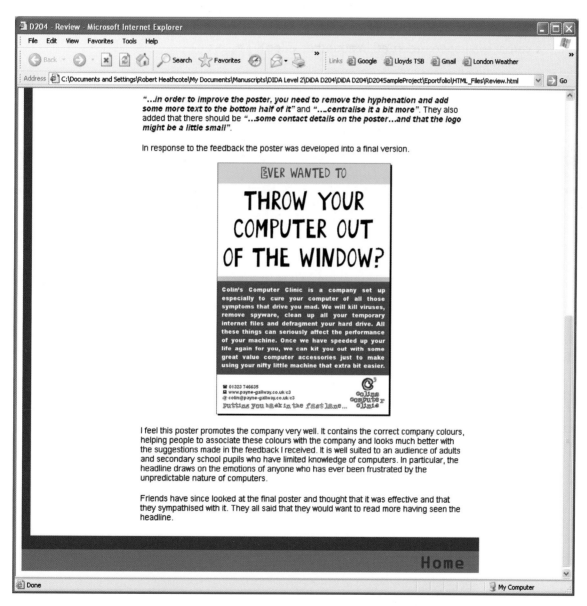

Figure 20.3: The final draft in the Review page of the Eportfolio

Chapter 20 – Review and evaluation

Making it interesting!

The review section can be very long and tiring for the examiner to read. The more you can engage the moderator the better chance you have of getting each point across effectively.

There is a variety of ways you can do this, or you can use a combination of each of them:

- a word-processed report
- a verbal evaluation recorded in sound or video
- a presentation
- graphics.

Good Marks... ✓

You will get good marks if you:

- have used the information in the SPB to write your review
- have used your diary and meeting records to explain the development of your work
- have made comments on the final outcomes of everything, including the eportfolio
- have made comments on your own performance, including your own contribution to the team
- have discussed improvements you would make if you had time.

Bad Marks... ✗

You will lose marks if you:

- have forgotten to include feedback from others in your review
- have not tested the links to the Review pages and they don't work.

Index

Index